NEWMAN: A MAN FOR OUR TIME

· CENTENARY ESSAYS ·

NEWMAN
A Man for Our Time

Henry Chadwick · Francesco Cossiga · Eric D'Arcy
Roy Jenkins · Anthony Kenny · David Newsome
Lord St John of Fawsley · Robert Runcie
A N Wilson

Edited by
DAVID BROWN

S·P·C·K

First published in Great Britain 1990
SPCK
Holy Trinity Church
Marylebone Road
London NW1 4DU

*Cataloguing in Publication Data
is available from the British Library*

ISBN 0 281 04486 4

Typeset by Pioneer Associates, Perthshire
Printed in Great Britain by
Dotesios Printers Ltd, Trowbridge, Wiltshire

Contents

Contributors

Dr David Brown Fellow, Chaplain and Tutor in Theology and Philosophy at Oriel College, Oxford, 1976–90; appointed Van Mildert Professor of Divinity in the University of Durham from October 1990. The author of a number of books on Christian ethics and philosophical theology, most recently *Invitation to Theology* (1989).

His Excellency Francesco Cossiga A former professor of constitutional law at the University of Sassari in Sardinia, he was elected a Member of the Italian Parliament in 1958. A former Minister of Home Affairs, he was elected President of the Senate in 1983 and President of the Italian Republic in 1985. He is an Honorary Fellow of Oriel College, Oxford.

Lord St John of Fawsley Author, barrister and journalist; Chairman of the Royal Fine Art Commission since 1985. Former President of the Cambridge Union (1950); MP for Chelmsford, 1964–87; Leader of the House of Commons, 1979–81. His publications include several books on the relation between law and morality, and he has edited *The Literary Works of Walter Bagehot* in fifteen volumes.

Dr David Newsome Fellow and Tutor in History at Emmanuel College, Cambridge, 1959–70; Headmaster of Christ's Hospital, 1970–9; Master of Wellington College, 1980–9. His publications include *The Parting of Friends* (1966), *Two Classes of Men* (1974) and *A. C. Benson the Diarist* (1980), which won the Whitbread Book of the Year Award.

Professor Henry Chadwick Master of Peterhouse, Cambridge, since 1987; Regius Professor of Divinity at Oxford, 1959–69; Dean of Christ Church, Oxford, 1969–79; Regius Professor of Divinity at Cambridge, 1979–83; member of ARCIC since 1969. His publications include *The Early Church* (1967) and editions of Origen's *Contra Celsum* and Lessing's *Theological Writings*.

The Most Revd Eric D'Arcy Archbishop of Hobart, Tasmania, since 1988. A former philosophy tutor at Melbourne University and author of an influential book, *Conscience and its Right to Freedom* (1961), he was

vii

Bishop of Sale immediately prior to his present appointment. He is also a member of two dicasteries of the Vatican Curia, those charged with responsibility for Catholic Education and Dialogue with Non-Believers.

Dr Anthony Kenny Warden of Rhodes House, Oxford, since 1989 and Professorial Fellow of St John's College, Oxford; Master of Balliol, 1978–89. His publications include *The Five Ways* (1969), *The God of the Philosophers* (1979), *Wyclif* (1985) and *Reason and Religion* (1987). He is currently President of the British Academy.

A N Wilson Novelist and biographer. His novels include *The Sweets of Pimlico* (John Llewellyn Rhys Memorial prize 1978), *The Healing Art* (Somerset Maugham Award, 1981) and *Incline Our Hearts* (1988); he has also written biographies of Hilaire Belloc, C S Lewis, Milton, Scott and Tolstoy. His *John Henry Newman: Prayers, Poems, Meditations* was published by SPCK in 1989.

Lord Jenkins of Hillhead Chancellor of the University of Oxford since 1987; Labour MP for Stechford, Birmingham, 1950–76; Chancellor of the Exchequer, 1967–70; President of the European Commission, 1977–81; SDP/Alliance MP for Glasgow, Hillhead, 1982–87. In addition to writings on current political issues, his publications include biographies of Attlee, Asquith, Baldwin and Truman.

The Most Revd Robert Runcie Archbishop of Canterbury 1980–91. A former undergraduate of Brasenose College, Oxford, he was successively Fellow and Dean of Trinity Hall (1956–60), Principal of Cuddesdon Theological College (1960–9) and Bishop of St Albans (1970–80).

Introduction

DAVID BROWN

John Henry Newman died at the grand old age of eighty-nine on 11 August 1890. The obituaries in the papers next day were profuse in their tributes to him. For instance *The Times* opened with the comment that 'a great man has passed away, a great link with the past has been broken', while *The Daily Telegraph* spoke of him as 'one of the most distinguished and highly gifted Englishmen of the nineteenth century'. No less eulogistic were the provincial press. The *Sussex Daily News* began its piece by declaring that 'a great Englishman and another of the saints has passed to his peace'; the *Liverpool Mercury* avowed that 'the death of Cardinal Newman deprives us of one of the greatest of Englishmen', while even in the far north in the heartlands of Presbyterian Scotland the *Aberdeen Evening Express* devoted a long article to him, the last paragraph of which contains the following glowing tribute: 'In the death of Cardinal Newman, one of the most outstanding personalities of the century has passed away. By his writings, as much as by his severance from the Church of England, followed by a long and saintly life, Newman has exercised an influence on the religious life of the country that is well-nigh incalculable.'[1]

It is a measure of the role he played in transforming the status of Roman Catholicism in England that a week later when his funeral took place *The Times* reported that 'in the neighbourhood of the Oratory alone the crowd must have numbered nearly 20,000 persons'. That transformation was fully acknowledged by *The Tablet*: 'As "our greatest witness for the faith", as a constant teacher by voice and pen and conduct, Cardinal Newman, during the last five and forty years, has done a greater work than change the form of a creed which was already in a state of solution . . . He has clothed Catholic philosophy and Catholic doctrine with a familiar garb, and set them both to the large music of our English speech.' As might have been expected, the religious weeklies of the other denominations were more cautious in their praise. None the less in a world before ecumenism it is remarkable how glowing the tributes in fact were. In the view of the *Methodist Recorder* 'by multitudes who rejected the peculiarities of his teaching he will be remembered as a great and a good man', while the weekly oracle of Evangelical Anglican opinion, *The Record*, balanced critique with praise: 'The secret of Newman's errors was his impatience of uncertainty, his craving for a basis of authority for the belief which he could not achieve by intellectual effort . . . But for all that there was a depth of spirituality and a personal piety obvious in every word and deed.' Somewhat surprisingly it was the *Church Times*, the voice of Anglo-Catholic opinion, which gave the most negative verdict on Newman's long-term significance. For, though its editorial ended by declaring that he had the character of a 'saint', it had begun by observing that 'Newman's influence has already waned, and will not, we think, much outlive this generation'.[2]

Fortunately, that last comment has proved to have been very wide of the mark. Within his adopted communion of Rome Newman's reputation has been steadily growing, especially since the Second Vatican Council (1962–5) and perhaps has never stood higher, while within the Church of England there is an increasing readiness to take his ideas seriously, despite his apparent 'desertion'. There was thus no hesitation at Oxford on the part of his two colleges – Trinity where he had been an undergraduate (1817–20) and Oriel where he had been a Fellow (1822–45) – that they too should mark the centenary of his death in some appropriate way.

From the University's point of view, however, Newman had died at a most inconvenient time – in the depths of the summer vacation – and so, although both the President of Trinity and the Provost of Oriel had attended his funeral in 1890, a century later it was thought best to move the principal Oxford celebrations to the Hilary Term (January to March), the following term being judged too near all the attendant pressures of university examinations. Seven public lectures were organized to reflect the range of Newman's concerns, culminating in the eighth and final week of the term with an ecumenical service in the University Church of St Mary the Virgin, of which Newman had himself been Vicar (1828–43).

The University is now a very different place from the institution Newman knew. When he left Oxford in 1845 it was still exclusively Anglican; now it is open to those of any faith or none. Then a reasonable familiarity with theology could be presumed; now that is no longer the case. These lectures reflect this different world. Anglicans, Roman Catholics and agnostics were all asked to contribute, and the organizers in their invitation stressed the importance of easy accessibility for a general audience. The reader can judge the result for him or herself, but certainly the verdict of those present was that the lecturers admirably fulfilled their remit. In a university like Oxford in which lectures are not compulsory it is commonplace to observe numbers attending them dwindle from a hundred or so at the first lecture in a series to a mere handful by the end. But in this case they remained constant throughout at between five and six hundred – as much a tribute to the quality of the lecturers as to Newman himself.

Apart from the inevitable alterations of style required by a written context and the provision of footnotes, the lectures are here presented almost exactly as they were delivered. A brief introductory paragraph at the beginning of each lecture has, however, been added by the editor to help orientate the reader. Inevitably in a series such as this in which the lecturers wrote without knowledge of what the other contributors intended to say, certain gaps have emerged. I would like therefore to use the rest of this Introduction to bring into sharper focus certain features of Newman's thought which, it seems to me, will ensure his increasing relevance for theological discussion and the future history of the Church. These are: his innovative ideas on development in doctrine; his refusal to treat theology as a complete or closed 'system'; his ecumenical significance; and, last but not least, his own personal pursuit of holiness.

I

Perhaps the most important contribution he made was his acceptance of the necessity of change within the Church. Religion is an aspect of life in which we all desire familiar landmarks. If it is truly the framework in terms of which we seek to live our lives, then

3

nothing could scarcely be more unsettling than to find that not only are our lives in constant change but that even the framework itself is not immune. In any case it surely sounds strange to suggest that a changeless God would impose a changing pattern upon our understanding of him and his purposes for ourselves and his Church. Yet it is part of Newman's achievement that he succeeded in reconciling his fellow Christians to this fact of change, perhaps primarily because he sought to do so in a way which does not threaten underlying, eternal truths.

It is this which sets him firmly apart from many of the advocates of change in the contemporary Church. For, properly to understand Newman's attitude, it needs to be set firmly in the context both of his strong belief in Providence and his attacks on 'Liberalism'. For Newman change is a divinely given means of bringing the Church to a fuller understanding of the truth, as well as enabling it to adapt to changed circumstances. He is thus totally opposed to any notion of the relativity of truth, and this is in fact what he means when he condemns 'Liberalism'. 'Liberalism in religion is the doctrine that there is no positive truth in religion, but that one creed is as good as another . . . It is inconsistent with any recognition of any religion as *true*. It teaches that all are to be tolerated, for all are matters of opinion.'[3]

Though there was some anticipation of his final position during his Anglican period, it is only with the *Essay on the Development of Christian Doctrine* of 1845, written to justify his imminent conversion to Rome, that one finds him enthusiastically endorsing a dynamic, developmental account. Yet, as Owen Chadwick among others has argued,[4] the permanent significance of this work – 'the most important single idea which Newman contributed to the thought of the Christian Church'[5] – lies neither in the fact that he was the first to propose the idea nor in the various tests which he offers for a true development, but in the seriousness with which he requires the Church to face the question of history. Hitherto notions of development had amounted to little more than the idea of logical inferences from already existing data, whereas Newman insisted that only particular historical circumstances made particular developments possible.

'In a higher world it is otherwise; but here below to live is to change, and to be perfect is to have changed often.'[6] That is the most famous sentence in the *Essay*, and well illustrates the fact that despite his own description of it as 'undoubtedly an hypothesis to account for a difficulty',[7] the theory of development is really very much more. For Newman it is in fact the normal pattern of God's relation towards us in this world. He asks elsewhere: 'What is the peculiarity of our nature, in contrast to the inferior animals around us?', and answers: 'Other beings are complete from their first existence, in that line of excellence which is allotted to them; but man begins with nothing realised . . . Thus he gradually advances to the fulness of his original destiny . . . It is his gift to be the creator of his own sufficiency; and to be emphatically self-made. This is the law of his being, which he cannot escape.'[8]

It is perhaps for this reason that he found it so easy to accept the conclusions of Darwin. Writing a couple of years after the publication of *The Origin of Species*, in one of his notebooks he observes critically of the traditional account: 'There is as much want of simplicity in the idea of the creation of distinct species as in those of the creation of trees in full growth or of rocks with fossils in them. I mean that it is as strange that monkeys should be so like men, with no historical connexion between them, as that there should be, or the notion that there was, no history or course of facts by which fossil bones got into the rocks . . . I will either go the whole hog with Darwin, or, dispensing with time and history altogether, hold, not only the theory of distinct species, but that also of the creation of the fossil-bearing rocks.'[9] Given the reference to 'dispensing with time and history altogether' (so unlike Newman), one suspects that the former is very much his real view and the latter option only entertained in case it should be required out of deference to ecclesiastical authority.

Though Newman's ideas on development have come all but universally to be seen as essential to any adequate account of church history, that reference to Genesis reminds us that similar questions can be, and are being, raised in respect of the Bible itself. Here, as yet, there is still no general agreement about the extent of legitimate application of Newman's basic principle. Already in his Anglican sermons Newman was wrestling with this question. For instance, in one of the *Parochial and Plain Sermons* he writes: 'The principle under consideration is this: that, whereas . . . all God is and does is absolutely perfect and complete, independent of time and place, . . . yet that in his actual dealings with the world that is, in all in which we see his Providence . . . , he seems to work by a

5

process, by means and ends, by steps, by victories hardly gained, and failures repaired and sacrifices ventured.'[10] In that sermon he takes justification by faith as an example; in a later one the sanctity of marriage.[11]

It was an issue with which he continued to wrestle even in the last decade of his life, producing, as he did in 1884, two articles on the inspiration of Scripture. In these he shows a commendable concern to limit inspirational claims for the Bible to faith and morals, and even then to make the inspiration indirect and mediated through the personality of the author. So for instance the Counter-Reformation Council of Trent's phrase 'Deus unus et idem utriusque Testamenti Auctor' is interpreted to mean that God is the 'originator', not the 'author', of both Testaments.[12] Again, he has no hesitation in accepting multiple authorship of the Pentateuch[13] or the fact that Scripture may err on matters other than faith and morals, as for example in his amusing instance of where Paul left his cloak.[14]

Yet even so in the light of the more advanced biblical studies of our day the questions need to be pushed further. Throughout his life Newman had a very patristic (Alexandrian) approach to the Scriptures that today would find few adherents among professional scholars.[15] We now know for instance that it is unlikely that Jesus ever explicitly claimed to be God; rather it was only gradually that the early Church came to a recognition of his divinity in the light of his resurrection, this culminating in the last Gospel to be written, that of St John, with its marvellous opening declaration of Jesus as God. Or, to take a very different instance, the structure of the Christian ministry is only gradually taking shape in the New Testament, with 'apostle', 'bishop' 'priest' and 'deacon' all having rather fluid meanings in the earlier material. But in neither case (or in any other case) should we suppose that 'earlier' means 'truer to the divine mind', unless we are prepared to dispense with the notion of divine providence altogether.

Of course, some criteria for determining what are and what are not legitimate developments would still be required. Clearly this is not the place to discuss them. My point is simply that, just as Newman succeeded in reconciling the Church of his own day to its own changing history, so in our own day his ideas may be used to reconcile ourselves to development within the Scriptures, as distinct from seeing them as a single, unchanging deposit. There is surely in any case a certain intuitive plausibility about this type of approach.

6

It would take time for the small, incipient, community to reflect upon the implications for its structures of becoming a universal Church; still more so, for the disciples to realize the stupendous fact that not only was this man God in their midst, he went voluntarily to a horrendous death for their sakes (and ours).

Though the contrast between the Old and New Testament is generally acknowledged, undoubtedly one reason why acceptance of such an approach within the New has been slow in coming is the radical failure of the first serious attempt to apply Newman's principles to the Bible in the Modernist controversy at the beginning of this century. Its leading exponent in France, Alfred Loisy, said of Newman that he was 'the most open-minded theologian to have existed in the Church since Origen', while George Tyrrell in England tried hard to associate Newman in the condemnation of their views in the papal encyclical *Pascendi* of 1907. Yet, though they were clearly influenced initially by Newman, there is no doubt that their final position stands at an enormous distance from his own. For instance both Loisy and Tyrrell sat lightly to doctrines, preferring instead to talk of 'poetry' and 'images', and both found the notion of miracle difficult to accept. What both adopted from Newman was a vague belief in progress, whereas for Newman himself, as we have seen, this had a very definite providential rationale, with nothing from the past jettisoned but rather caught up into a richer understanding of the divine reality.

II

Not only that, the Modernists failed to appreciate the reasons why Newman thought such gradualism inevitable, reasons which also explain his hostility to the very notion of system in theology. Newman's reference in the *Apologia* to resting 'in the thought of two and two only absolute and luminously self-evident beings, myself and my Creator'[16] sometimes misleads readers into believing that Newman was guilty of a rather pernicious and extreme form of individualism. But, as his sermons make clear, what is really at stake is Newman's concern for a truly personal relationship with God, in which all human beings can share. But, while the relationship can be deep, there is, in his view, no corresponding capacity for encapsulating in thought the fulness of the divine vision. It is necessarily fragmentary and limited, though it can grow with time.

Newman draws on a series of brilliant images to hammer his point home. For instance of our conception of God he writes: 'We can indeed combine the various matters which we know of him by an act of intellect, and treat them theologically, but such theological combinations are no objects for the imagination to gaze upon. Our image of him never is one, but broken into numberless partial aspects, independent of each. As we cannot see the whole starry firmament at once, but have to turn ourselves from east to west, and then round to east again, sighting first one constellation and then another, and losing these in order to gain those, so it is, and much more, with such real apprehensions as we can secure of the divine nature.'[17] Initially this passage from *The Grammar of Assent* may seem to be in flat contradiction to what he says in the *University Sermons* of the sense of unity which we gain from our impression of the divine: 'As God is one, so the impression he gives of himself is one; it is not a thing of parts; it is not a system . . . It is the vision of an object. When we pray, we pray, not to an assemblage of notions, or to a creed, but to one individual being; and when we speak of him we speak of a person, not of a law or manifestation.'[18] Yet there is no real conflict. When we pray we are conscious of being in relation to one single personal being, but when we attempt to combine all the different images we have of that being into a single whole, it proves beyond our powers to systematize them all into a coherent whole. The system, though it succeeds in part, none the less remains less than its constituent parts.

For some this would be taken to show the incoherence of the concept, but for Newman what it demonstrates is the limitations of our formal reasoning faculties. As he remarks of the Trinity: 'Break a ray of light into its constituent colours; each is beautiful, each may be enjoyed; attempt to unite them, and perhaps you produce only a dirty white. The pure and indivisible Light is seen only by the blessed inhabitants of heaven; here we have but faint reflections of it as its diffraction supplies; but they are sufficient for faith and devotion. Attempt to combine them into one, and you gain nothing but a mystery, which you can describe as a notion, but cannot depict as an imagination.'[19] As Newman puts it in a famous contrast, while it is in principle possible to give 'systematic' expression to a doctrine of the Trinity, all the assent one could give to this would be purely formal or 'notional', not the kind of 'real assent' which engages the imagination and shows that one has full comprehension of what is meant. 'Religion has to do with the real, and the real is the particular; theology has to do with the notional, and the notional is general and systematic.'[20]

Newman leaves us in no doubt about the reasons for such limitations: 'Partial and incomplete knowledge must surely be an inseparable attendant on a theology which reveals the wonders of heaven. The human mind cannot measure the things of the Spirit. Christianity is a supernatural gift, originating and living in the unseen world and only extending into this. It is a vast scheme running out into width and breadth, encompassing us round about, not embraced by us. No one can see the form of a building but those who are external to it. We are within the divine dispensation; we cannot take it in with the eye, ascertain its proportions, pursue its lines, foretell its directions and coincidences, or ascertain their limits.'[21]

But that very tantalizing incompleteness is used by Newman to explain why developments in understanding are possible; the building, though still seen only partially, is now viewed from a different, and thus possibly more illuminating perspective; or, to use an image found in the *Essay on Development,* some of the varied terrain is now more clearly seen. That landscape image Newman had already used in an essay of 1835, and there, perhaps more powerfully than anywhere else, he exhibits his understanding of the hidden potentials of Scripture, at the same time warning against any self-confident assurance of bringing them all to completion. 'No revelation can be complete and systematic, from the weakness of the human intellect; so far as it is not such, it is mysterious. When nothing is revealed, nothing is known, and there is nothing to contemplate or marvel at; but when something is revealed, and only something, for all cannot be, there are forthwith difficulties and perplexities. A Revelation is religious doctrine viewed on its illuminated side; a mystery is the selfsame doctrine viewed on the side unilluminated. Thus religious truth is neither light nor darkness, but both together; it is like the dim view of a country seen in the twilight, which forms half extricated from the darkness, with broken lines and isolated masses. Revelation, in this way of considering it, is not a revealed system, but consists of a number of detached and incomplete truths belonging to a vast system unrevealed, of doctrines and injunctions mysteriously connected together; that is, connected by unknown media, and bearing upon unknown portions of the system.'[22]

So far from representing irrationalism such remarks of Newman constitute a wise reminder of the limits of human reason, and one as necessary today as in his own lifetime. It is so easy to fall prey to the temptation to 'plug the gaps', to assume that the interconnections between the various Christian doctrines must be known to us. The result is often logical interconnectedness at the price of triviality or worse, as in the morally outrageous reasons which are sometimes given to account for the necessity of Christ's death. By contrast Newman wisely insists on an admission of ignorance; 'Why was this suffering necessary to procure the blessings which we were in ourselves unworthy of? We do not know.'[23] In similar vein in the Preface to the third edition of the *Via Media*, rather than arguing for some necessary hierarchy between 'prophet' (theology), 'priest' (religion) and 'king' (authority), he insists upon a subtle, unquantifiable interplay between them.

A similar attitude is also to be found in his approach to the question of proofs of the existence of God. The traditional arguments are given short shrift, while even his frequent, favoured appeals to conscience are never assigned the status of demonstrations. Instead of strict deduction, he maintains, the general pattern of human rationality has a much more loose, informal character, and in this the justification of religious belief is no exception. Such is the argument of both his Anglican *University Sermons* and his later *Grammar of Assent*. For long his approach was ignored and claims for the deductive validity of the traditional arguments continued to be made to an unbelieving world. But more recently philosophers of religion in Britain and the United States have moved much closer to Newman's conception. One such is Basil Mitchell, whose influential book, *The Justification of Religious Belief* (1973), breathes the spirit of Newman, though he only explicitly quotes him once. For both writers justification is 'the cumulation of probabilities . . . probabilities too fine to avail separately, too subtle and circuitous to be convertible into syllogisms'.[24] His successor in the chair at Oxford, Richard Swinburne, has continued this inductive approach though with a scientific rigour which Newman would have deemed impossible. An eagerly awaited contribution to this debate is promised in print shortly from America's leading philosopher of religion, Alvin Plantinga. To judge by versions given so far in lectures, this is likely to have some marked similarities to Newman's own position. Once again, there are likely to be few, if any, explicit references. Newman's style is so unlike that of the modern, analytical philosopher that there is no natural meeting of minds, however similar the ultimate content of the thought might be. We are therefore particularly fortunate in this volume to have a presentation of Newman through the eyes of as distinguished an analytical philosopher as Anthony Kenny. For his contribution could make the parallels with Newman more widely known.

III

If Newman's influence in this respect is as yet largely unrealized, the same cannot be said for his impact on ecumenical relations. Born an Anglican in 1801 and a convert to Rome in 1845, his death in 1890 meant that he had spent exactly half his life in each communion. It is hard to exaggerate the transformation he helped bring about in both, in each case drawing the one closer to the other.

In the case of the Church of England this impact was of course felt through the Oxford Movement, of which he was the principal intellectual leader. Though Anglo-Catholics often see themselves as the exclusive heirs of that movement, every aspect of the Church was in fact affected. Nowadays even most Evangelical parishes would have Holy Communion as their main service; their choirs would be robed, and they would raise no objection when the bishop appears wearing a mitre. In this illustration I have deliberately mixed the trivial with the profound; for both affect the 'feel' of what it is to be an Anglican, and both can ultimately be traced to the influence of that movement. In the early nineteenth century in the typical parish Sacrament Sunday would only have occurred a mere three or four times a year; by 1837 Newman as Vicar of St Mary's had succeeded in establishing a weekly celebration of the Eucharist. Again, prior to Bishop Edward King, an erstwhile undergraduate of Oriel, no Anglican bishop had worn a mitre since the Reformation.

But one should by no means confine such influence to the practice of the faith. It was the condemnation of Newman's interpretation of the Thirty-Nine Articles in Tract 90 which gave the final spur to Newman's move towards Rome. Yet today it is inconceivable that there could be a successful prosecution on this score, so firmly entrenched is his reading as a legitimate doctrinal position within the Church of England (however implausible this may be as an account of the compilers' original intentions!). Indeed, one even finds a former Archbishop of Canterbury writing in his defence.[25]

That same Archbishop has spoken of Newman's 'wonderful nearness to the New Testament'.[26] That surely must be noted as one of the great legacies he brought to his adopted Church.[27] His sermons abound in biblical references; indeed they sometimes put the average reader to a severe test, particularly in their wealth of Old Testament allusions. Roman Catholicism in the nineteenth century was in danger of degenerating into a rather narrow scholasticism. The Second Vatican Council (1962–5) changed all that, and, as Lord St John observes in his lecture, no less a figure than Paul VI called it 'Newman's Council'. That it most certainly was in respect of Rome's approach to the Bible. Not only has there been a tremendous flourishing of biblical studies; many of the internationally most distinguished scholars, such as Raymond Brown, are Roman Catholics.

Assessing the extent of Newman's direct influence upon that Council is no easy matter. Some of those present were certainly greatly influenced by him. Cardinal Willebrands, for instance, had written his doctorate on Newman, while Archbishop Worlock organized a seminar during the Council on Newman's view on the role of the laity. On the other hand, it is unlikely that he exercised any major role in recovering for Rome a more biblically inspired theology. Indeed, Bishop Butler is probably right that it was less a case of direct impact, and much more of Newman 'possessing a sort of prophetic charisma'[28] about the direction Rome would eventually take. But, whether as antecedent influence or as answering echo, there is no doubt that very many of the leading ideas of Vatican II are those of Newman.

Apart from the centrality of Scripture and the notion of development, his other leading idea which finds a clear response in Vatican II is his treatment of the role of the laity. Newman's essay in the *Rambler* of 1859 'On Consulting the Faithful in Matters of Doctrine', like his famous later remark that he would drink 'to Conscience first, and to the Pope afterwards',[29] though not intended as attacks on the hierarchy, were certainly meant to exclude exaggerated pretensions on its behalf. Indeed with remarkable

12

foresight Newman predicted that the declaration of papal infallibility at Vatican I in 1870 would one day find its appropriate counter-balance: 'If you look into history, you find Popes continually completing the acts of their predecessors, and Councils too – sometimes only half the truth is brought out at one time – I doubt not a coming Pope or a coming Council will so explain and guard what has now been passed by the late Council, as to clear up all that troubles us now.'[30] That expectation has surely been admirably fulfilled in Vatican II, with its insistence that the Pope only speaks infallibly when he expresses the mind of the whole Church. Little wonder that it has become possible for a subsequent archbishop, Dr Runcie, to express hope for reunion of the two Churches under a shared papacy.

There are thus a number of Newman's ideas drawing the two Churches together, particularly with Canterbury's increased stress on the sacramental character of the Church and Rome's on the biblical witness of the whole people of God. Not only that, may not Newman's theory of development be used to ease at least some of the doctrinal disputes between the two Communions? It would be a case of neither Church having a vision of the whole landscape, but each requiring the other's partial outlook in order to form a more complete picture. A case in point might be the doctrine of justification by faith. In his *Lectures on Justification* of 1838 Newman argued that the Anglican position represented a *via media* between the Roman and extreme Protestant. As a historical claim, the thesis has numerous critics.[31] He seems to have misrepresented theologians of both the Reformation and the Counter-Reformation. None the less as an account of how each popularly conceived the other he is very close to target: Protestants of his day did tend to think of Roman Catholics as supposing that salvation was entirely a matter of works, while equally popular Protestantism did often sound as though it were demanding that one work oneself into an emotional state of commitment (hence, no doubt, the reason why such emotions are so frequently the object of attack in Newman's sermons).[32] By contrast in a passage like the following Newman offers us the perfect balance between the two extremes: 'It is the Divine Presence that justifies us, not faith, as say the Protestant schools, not renewal, as say the Romans. The word of justification is the substantive living Word of God, entering the soul, illuminating and cleansing it, as fire brightens and purifies material substances.'[33]

Justification is thus a matter neither of our producing the emotional commitment of faith nor of our justifying ourselves by our actions, but of God's giving us both faith and works through his indwelling Spirit transforming us. But note that Newman obtains this result not by excluding one or other of the two extremes, but by incorporating them both into a deeper understanding.

IV

Earlier in this Introduction we have already noticed the way in which Newman commonly esteemed system in theology less highly than the personal character of religion. Certainly he held his views on justification with such firmness, not primarily for intellectual reasons, but precisely because he saw the life of the spirit at stake. The 'Catholic' view seemed to interpose a great distance between God and man, to be bridged by 'works', whereas for Newman the unseen world was ever close about us: 'Every breath of air and ray of light and heat, every beautiful prospect, is, as it were, the skirts of their garments, the waving of the robes of those whose faces see God in heaven.'[34] But, if one must choose which of the two was seen as the more threatening, it was the 'Protestant' view; for it seemed to imply that our relation with God was an all or nothing affair. We had either once and for all made the decision or not, and that was all that counted, whereas for Newman it was a matter of a lifetime's gradual growth into holiness under the indwelling guidance of God.

That emphasis on the gradualness of change is evident throughout his sermons. For instance preaching on 'Sudden Conversions' he remarks: 'When men change their religious opinions really and truly, it is not merely their opinions that they change, but their hearts; and this evidently is not done in a moment – it is a slow work.'[35] It is only through continual practice in good works and in prayer that the right kind of inward disposition can be created: 'Outward acts, done on principle, create inward habits.'[36] So 'good works . . . are required, not as if they had any merit in them, not as if they could of themselves turn away God's anger for our sins', but because they 'will be the means of making our hearts holy, and of preparing us for the future presence of God'.[37] Again, novelty in prayer is repeatedly attacked and the value of routine stressed, since human beings require 'the necessity of humble, tedious practice to enable them to pray effectively'. Novelty merely postpones the

14

problem, whereas periods of distraction are inevitable until a habit has become deeply formed. 'For no habit is formed at once; and before the flame of religion in the heart is purified and strengthened by long practice and experience, of course it will be capricious in its motions, it will flare about and flicker, and at times seem almost to go out.'[38]

Debate continues to rage about the sense in which it is appropriate, if at all, to describe Newman as a saint. In the pages that follow one will find both unstinted praise and some severe criticisms. Certainly in some of his dealings with others, for instance the London Oratory, he seems to have been unduly 'prickly'; as Keble remarked of him, he was 'a very sensitive person'.[39] What makes this particularly ironical is that the treatment he metes out to others in his writings is often biting and caustic. A recent biographer has spoken of 'superb snubs' and 'superb sneers',[40] but it is hard not to judge many of them grossly unfair and uncharitable. To question, for instance, Dr Arnold's commitment to Christianity was simply a travesty of the truth. But at the same time it should be noted that one modern attempt by a Roman Catholic priest to convict Newman of systematic dishonesty has singularly failed to win general assent.[41]

But even to put the question in this way is surely to misjudge the nature of sanctity. To declare someone a saint is not to declare them without faults; it is in fact all too easy a matter to identify deficiencies of character in most of those already canonized. What makes a saint is their lively sense of the presence of God and their absolute determination to strive towards the Christian ideal, fallen creatures though they are. By this test Newman succeeds admirably. No one can read his sermons without being convinced that here was a man struggling with all his might to be conformed by God's grace to the image of his Lord, and in the process giving us insights of permanent value into the nature of that spiritual struggle.

No wonder that Dean Church said of his sermons that 'they were the expression of a piercing and large insight into character and conscience and motives'.[42] Again and again the reader finds himself convicted by Newman's perceptivity, of the numerous ways in which we deceive ourselves or are corrupted by apparently trivial beginnings.[43] Yet what gives them even greater power is the realization that Newman is looking not just into others' hearts, but also into his own. It is impossible for instance not to read his repeated call for a return to childlike innocence[44] as anything other than an attack on his own sophistication; or his insistence that love must begin with family and friends[45] as other than a self-addressed sermon on his often difficult relationships with his brothers and colleagues. Even the brilliant stylist that he was does not find himself immune.[46]

In this centenary year the Pope may choose to beatify or canonize Newman, and rightly so in my view. But I write as an Anglican. The nearest equivalent procedures in the Church of England are constituted by inclusion in the list of 'Lesser Festivals and Commemorations' at the beginning of *The Alternative Service Book*. One representative of the Oxford Movement is already there (John Keble). But so too are several post-Reformation Roman Catholics, among them Francis de Sales, Vincent de Paul, Teresa of Avila and John of the Cross, as well as non-Anglican Protestants such as John Bunyan. Even John Wesley finds a mention, despite the fact that it was his ordination of one of his followers in violation of episcopal rules which led to the severance of Methodism from the Church of England. If Wesley can be forgiven, why not then Newman? In retrospect not only has no man in the past two centuries done more to give the two Churches a common vision of themselves, it was a common vision born of the pursuit of a life of holiness.

It is to a consideration of the nature of that life that we now turn.

NOTES

1. All from editions on 12 August 1890.
2. *The Times*, 20 August; *Tablet*, 23 August; *Methodist Recorder*, 14 August; *Record*, 15 August; *Church Times*, 15 August.
3. From his speech on his elevation to the cardinalate in 1879: W Ward, *Life of John Henry Cardinal Newman* (Longmans 1912), vol. II, p. 460.
4. O Chadwick, *From Bossuet to Newman* (Cambridge University Press 1957).
5. O Chadwick, *Newman* (Oxford University Press 1983), p. 48.
6. *Essay on Development* (Penguin 1973), ch. 1, sec. 1; p. 100.
7. ibid., Introduction, p. 90.
8. *Grammar of Assent* (New York, Doubleday, 1955), ch. 9, sec. 1; pp. 273–4.
9. Unpublished paper at Birmingham Oratory (Birmingham Oratory Archives A46.3; Book of Sundries, p. 83; 9 Dec. 1863).
10. *Parochial and Plain Sermons* (San Francisco, Ignatius Press, 1987), II, 8; p. 279.

11. ibid., II, 12; p. 308.
12. 'Inspiration in its Relation to Revelation', in *Newman on the Inspiration of Scripture*, ed. J D Holmes and R Murray (Geoffrey Chapman 1967), pp. 107–8.
13. ibid., p. 120.
14. Essay II in ibid., pp. 143–4 and 151.
15. An illustration of the contrast between Newman's day and our own is the way in which he assumes in *Parochial and Plain Sermons* that 'Son of God' is equivalent to an assertion of Christ's divinity (cf. III, 12; p. 581) – something no New Testament scholar would now do.
16. *Apologia* (Sheed & Ward 1976), p. 3.
17. *Grammar of Assent*, ch. 5, sec. 2; p. 116.
18. *University Sermons*, ed. D M MacKinnon and J D Holmes (SPCK 1970), XV, 21; p. 330.
19. *Grammar of Assent*, ch. 5, sec. 2; pp. 116–17.
20. ibid., p. 122.
21. *Via Media* (Longmans 1895), vol. I, pp. 89–90 (*Lectures on Prophetical Office*, III, 4).
22. *Essays Critical and Historical* (Longmans 1887), vol. I, pp. 41–2 (Essay 2, 4).
23. *Parochial and Plain Sermons*, I, 16; p. 131.
24. B Mitchell, *The Justification of Religious Belief* (Macmillan 1973), p. 51 (quoting *Grammar of Assent*, 8, 2; p. 230).
25. A M Ramsey, 'Newman the Anglican', in *John Henry Newman; A Man for our Time?*, ed. T R Wright (Newcastle upon Tyne, Grevatt & Grevatt 1983), pp. 4–5.
26. A M Ramsey, 'The Significance of Newman Today', in *The Rediscovery of Newman*, ed. J Coulson and A M Allchin (SPCK 1967), p. 8.
27. Bishop B C Butler, 'Newman and the Second Vatican Council', in ibid., pp. 235ff. lists 'a more biblical theology' as the first of seven obvious parallels between Newman and the Council.
28. ibid., p. 245.
29. *Letter to the Duke of Norfolk* (1875), sec. 5.
30. *Letters and Diaries*, ed. C S Dessain et al. (Oxford University Press), XXV, 322; cf. also 310.
31. e.g. A E McGrath, *Iustitia Dei* (Cambridge University Press 1986), vol. 2, pp. 121–34.
32. e.g. *Parochial and Plain Sermons*, VII, 10; p. 1484.
33. *Lectures on Justification* (Longmans 1892), VI, 10; p. 154.
34. *Parochial and Plain Sermons*, II, 29; p. 453.
35. ibid., VIII, 15; p. 1682.
36. ibid., I, 1; p. 10.
37. ibid., p. 9.
38. Both quotations, ibid., I, 11; p. 92.
39. Quoted in I Ker, *John Henry Newman: A Biography* (Oxford, Clarendon Press, 1988), p. 167.

40. ibid., pp. 87, 185. The former gives the reference to Arnold.
41. P J FitzPatrick, 'Newman's *Apologia*: Was Kingsley right?', in T R Wright, op. cit., pp. 28–36; and elsewhere.
42. R W Church, *The Oxford Movement* (University of Chicago Press 1970), p. 93.
43. e.g. *Parochial and Plain Sermons*, IV, 3 (pp. 750ff.); V, 14 (esp. pp. 1079ff.).
44. e.g. ibid., II, 6 (pp. 264ff.); V, 8 (pp. 1014ff.).
45. ibid., II, 5; pp. 257ff.
46. ibid., II, 30; pp. 457ff.

· 1 ·

Newman the Man

One of England's most distinguished Roman Catholic laymen and himself an admirer of Newman, Lord St John of Fawsley, opens the series with a character portrait of the man. But the influence of Newman is by no means confined to the English-speaking world, far less to his native land. His writings and personality are as much a source of attraction and fascination on the European mainland. As a preamble to Lord St John's more general portrait, it is therefore fitting that we should first have some account of the reasons for this widespread attraction. The fact that they are offered by no less a person than the President of the Italian Republic, one of Oriel's Honorary Fellows, gives clear evidence of the extent of such interest. He uses Newman's four visits to Italy as a clue to the reasons for this fascination.

NEWMAN AND ITALY

Francesco Cossiga

The Newman Conference which took place in Oriel in 1966 included a number of papers which examined Newman's influence on the European mainland, in France, Germany, and the Netherlands. I am not going to add another here on his influence in Italy, but, in offering a brief, introductory characterization, I would like to make use – perhaps a little arbitrarily – of his visits to Rome. The complexity of the impressions which the city made on him, can be seen to reflect the underlying, continuous complexity which he bore within himself and so may indicate for us reasons for the interest he still arouses among so many people.

I

Newman visited Rome on four occasions. He came first in 1833, during his Mediterranean holiday with the Froudes. It was a mixed experience, overshadowed by his solitary return visit to Sicily. Newman has always viewed the world and life itself as the stakes in an incessant struggle between light and darkness and this conflict he experienced in himself in Sicily. He was struck down by a serious illness, during which he was subject to a mysterious experience of a mystic nature: he underwent a struggle involving the soul, the devil, and God. It was then that he re-examined his whole life and saw it under the sign of Providence with which, despite short periods of discouragement, he had always tried to correspond. Thus he was able to exclaim: 'I shall not die, because I have not sinned against the light', and to recognize a providential call to his future mission: 'I have a work to do in England.' These sentiments of abandonment to God and hope found expression in his famous poem, 'Lead, kindly light', which he composed during his journey home.

Before this crisis, however, he had already been affected deeply at finding himself in Rome, where apostles and saints were martyred and buried. He was overcome by the extreme beauty and costliness of the churches and he saluted the city 'to which England owes the blessings of the Gospel'. At the same time, he recoiled from what he saw as superstitions, 'or rather', as he added, 'what is far worse, the solemn reception of them as an essential part of Christianity'.[1] Homeward bound and homesick three months later in Palermo, still convalescing from his illness, he composed another poem, 'The Good Samaritan', which begins:

> O that thy creed were sound!
> For thou dost soothe the heart, thou Church of Rome,
> By thy unwearied watch and varied round
> Of service, in thy Saviour's holy home.[2]

This first visit displays his alertness to complexity and ambiguity and his reluctance to tame it. All the same, he hoped never to travel abroad again.

II

He came back in 1846. By the time of his second visit, he had left the Church of England and been received into full communion with the Catholic Church. He went to Rome to prepare for his ordination to the priesthood and to search out the kind of priestly vocation to which he was best suited. Upon investigation, neither the Dominicans nor the Jesuits appealed to him, nor was he attracted by the newly founded Institute of Charity. On his way south, he stopped in Milan to meet Antonio Rosmini, its founder and the greatest Italian philosopher of the nineteenth century, but for a variety of reasons the meeting never took place. Before leaving England, however, Nicholas Wiseman, the future Cardinal, had encouraged him to consider the Oratorians. It was good advice.

The Oratorians had been founded by St Philip Neri in the sixteenth century. A Florentine, who combined an almost mystical spirituality with a sunny, outward-going disposition (similar to his English contemporary, Thomas More), Philip had come to Rome in 1533. As a layman, young people, attracted by his personality and style of life, had gathered around him. They met for the pleasure of each others' company, but also to pray. After seventeen years, Philip was persuaded to accept ordination to the priesthood and those gatherings of friends developed into the Congregation of the Oratory. His influence on Rome has earned him the title of its apostle for the late sixteenth century. What Newman discovered in the Oratory was something akin to an Oxford college. He had hoped to live and die a fellow of Oriel. That was not to be. But in the Oratory he found a kindred appreciation of home and stability, a rule of life, but without vows, and a flexibility which gave scope to his many pastoral interests, including his concern for education. He became an Oratorian, received permission to adapt the rule for English circumstances, and returned home to found the Congregation in Birmingham and later in London. This second visit was a time for discernment and creativity.

III

Newman's third visit to Rome took place in 1856. It was caused by a clash between those two Oratories which he had founded. That sad, old dispute is of no interest here, but the fact of Newman's coming to Rome tells us something about him. In an attempt to resolve the difficulty, he had acted. Gifted with a brilliant, creative mind, he has so often been dismissed in popular judgement as a dreamer, too passive and too lost in clouds of speculation ever to act. It is not true and this third visit can stand as an example of the practical side of his character, his vigour, his energy, and his administrative ability.

IV

And finally, Newman went to Rome in 1879 to receive his cardinal's hat. After a Catholic life filled with trials and often under a cloud of official suspicion, it was a moment of unexpected happiness and fulfilment. More important than the honour itself was the approval it signified, the cloud, as he said, lifted from him for ever. And at this point I should like to refer again to Rosmini[3] and the close connection between him and Newman.

It is certain that Newman respected and admired Rosmini; he too had lived under a cloud. In his private diary, Newman has strong words of condemnation for the way in which Rosmini had been treated by the ecclesiastical authorities. On the occasion of his death, writing from Dublin to the Superior General of the Institute of Charity, Fr Pagani, he asserted that Rosmini 'belonged to the whole Church', adding with an extremely human touch: 'I fear that the tribulations he suffered shortened his life.'[4]

Newman and Rosmini were two great masters who fought in defence of truth and Christianity. But, while their teaching coincided on many points, there were also differences. Both of them were Christian thinkers of depth and power. Faith for them, in other words, was not a substitute for reason, but itself a source of knowledge which enjoyed a delicate and complex alliance with reason. Anything less they saw as a threat to the integrity of Christian believing. Thus Rosmini, according to the title of one of his posthumously published works, opposed 'rationalism, that attempts to insinuate itself into the theological schools', and Newman, speaking in Rome in 1879, could point to his lifelong stand against liberalism, by which he meant 'the doctrine that there is no positive truth in religion, but that one creed is as good as another'. He had detected this tendency among the Noetics in the Oriel Senior Common Room in the 1820s, denounced it in his first major work, *The Arians of the Fourth Century*, and opposed it ever since.

However, while sharing the same basic Christian frame of reference, the character of their genius was distinct. Rosmini's was metaphysical, Newman's existential. Nevertheless, both gave priority to a concrete way of thinking. They prized reality, Rosmini in metaphysical speculation, Newman in psychological and existential inquiry. And this concern for reality – and indeed Christian reality – forced both of them to be sensitive to history. Here, perhaps, in the difficult question of the relationship between structure (thought), on the one hand, and history (Christianity), on the other, is the difference in their ways of thinking to be found. Their different interpretations of the problems of the world and history aside, however, Newman and Rosmini emerge today as two exalted spirits, two prophets and pioneers in the Church, who suffered for their love of truth.

But in what follows it is of course Newman who holds our attention. It is not possible to do him justice in so brief a space, but something of the reason why he still attracts so much interest may be gauged from these reflections, prompted by his visits to Rome. The man who has emerged is patient with ambiguity, discerning and creative, an energetic administrator, and an advocate of religious truth in all its complexity. And that is only the beginning.

NOTES

1. *Letters and Diaries*, iii, p. 238.
2. *Verses on Various Occasions*, 153.
3. Antonio Rosmini-Serbati (1797–1855) can in many ways be viewed as the Italian Newman, or indeed Newman as the English Rosmini. For both their lives were characterized by a concern for the Church to come to terms with the modern world, though this was set within a continued deep loyalty to her teachings. Thus, just as Newman for instance argued for the legitimacy of change and for an increased role for the laity, so Rosmini not only succeeded in injecting a strong Catholic element into the movement towards Italian unification but also developed a philosophy which, while remaining loyal to Augustine and Aquinas, took seriously the challenge of Kant. Like Newman too he fell under suspicion, being placed once on the Index during his life and once receiving papal censure after his death (though both were subsequently rescinded).
4. *Letters and Diaries*, xvi, pp. 504–5.

Newman: A Portrait

LORD ST JOHN OF FAWSLEY

The character of John Henry Newman, whose life almost literally spanned the nineteenth century, has always fascinated and perplexed. He baffled contemporaries while he intrigued them. On his death Lord Rosebery travelled to Birmingham to gaze for the last time on the face on which were etched the aspirations, problems and sufferings of a century of turmoil and change.

We from our more detached standpoint in time can, looking back, see him with some degree of objectivity. His luminous and subtle mind fascinates but we can perceive more clearly the essential simplicity of a man whose life centred entirely on God. He had an exceptional self-awareness but this should not be confused, as some have done, with self-centredness. His nature from the earliest years seems to have been extraordinarily susceptible to outside impressions, the memories of which remained with him throughout his long life. He could recall lying in his cradle at the age of four, watching the lights of candles reflected in the glass of the windows where they had been placed to celebrate the victory of Trafalgar in 1805. As a child his life of imagination and feeling was vibrant and was destined to be supplemented by the development of a soaring and vigorous power of intellect and a capacity for action and leadership. Although involved for long periods of his life in controversy and public life, he spent many years in the privacy of a community existence at the Birmingham Oratory. He interested himself not only in theology but in current affairs, which he followed closely and discerningly. For Ireland, which was to be the scene of his great but doomed battle to set up a Catholic university, he had a most unVictorian sympathy. He referred always, to what most contemporaries regarded as a desolate plague spot, as 'our beloved sister island' and in the 'fifties he scurried back and forth across the

24

often atrocious Irish sea in a vain attempt to bring the opportunities of a higher education to an unfortunate and deprived people.

One key to the understanding of Newman's character and influence is to perceive him as a balancing force. In his Anglican period he recalled the Church of England to her Catholic roots and championed her rights against the destructive liberalism of the day. In his Catholic period he stood out against the excesses of the ultramontane party led in England by Manning and Ward, arguing for a genuine pluralism within the wider all embracing unity of the Catholic Church. His ideas were regarded with detestation by the dominant church party of his period, but not by Pio Nono, and they had to wait until our own time to come into their own. Paul VI rightly described the Second Vatican Council as Newman's Council.

Although engaged in many controversies throughout his life, both inside and outside the Catholic Church, Newman maintained a remarkable inner serenity. 'One of the signs', he once wrote, 'of the presence of God is peace.'

Throughout his life Newman attached great importance to dates and anniversaries. He treasured them as affording peeps into the pattern in the carpet. One of the most significant for him was 14 December 1816 – the day chosen by John Newman, his father, then a prosperous banker, to secure university entrance for his clever eldest son John Henry, then two months short of sixteen. When John Henry was over seventy he wrote of the moment of departure as 'an illustration of the seeming accidents on which our course of life and personal history turn'.[1] Like Rosmini he had a very positive idea of 'divine Providence'. His father, who had not graduated from either university, had been (his son recalled) 'in doubt whether to direct the post-boy to make for Hounslow' (the Cambridge road) 'or for the first stage on the road to Oxford'. At this critical moment a family friend arrived, the curate of St James', Piccadilly, who successfully espoused the Oxford cause. He accompanied them, and after failing to get John Henry into his own old college, Exeter, succeeded in having him matriculated at Trinity College. When he returned to school his headmaster's reaction was, 'Trinity: a most gentlemanlike college – I am much pleased to hear it.' One asks oneself, could the Oxford movement have ever come from Cambridge? Another date always remembered was the 12th of April 1822, when he made up for his failure to gain honours in his degree by the award of a Fellowship at Oriel, the most intellectual college in an as yet unreformed university. Its high-thinking plain-living dons were supposed by other colleges to sit over tea in the evenings rather than claret. In 1874 when Newman was composing a memoir of his life up to 1830, couched in the third person, he wrote of that day as: 'the turning point of his life, and of all days most memorable'; and said that he was 'constant all through his life in his thoughtful remembrance year after year of this great mercy of Divine Providence, and of his electors, by whom it was brought about'.[2] There he made friends and received – and exercised – intellectual and spiritual influence. During his residence, he declared, 'the religious sentiment in his mind, which had been his blessing from the time he left school, was gradually developed and formed and brought to its legitimate issue'. That issue finally came in October 1845 when he resigned his Fellowship and was received into the Catholic Church. In February 1846 when he returned to Oxford to clear up the house at Littlemore where he had lived, self-exiled from Oriel, since 1842, he told the friend who had been his curate there: 'I quite tore myself away and could not help kissing my bed, and mantlepiece, and other parts of the house.'[3]

The gradual development and formation during the course of which his undergraduate teaching was taken from him, and he relinquished his university pulpit, is explained in his *History of my Religious Opinions* (the original title of the *Apologia*). That book could not have been written at all – let alone written at such speed and with unremitting labour night and day to get its weekly parts to the publisher – if Newman had not been able to draw on books, documents, letters to and from friends and colleagues, and his own diaries and memoranda. Throughout the second half of his life, he used spare intervals of time left from the demands of being Superior of the Birmingham Oratory, running its school, founding the Catholic University of Ireland, and other undertakings – in sorting and ordering his private memoranda and letters he had written (the latter returned or borrowed and transcribed). Sometimes he asked himself why he was taking the trouble, making such comments as: 'Things most interesting and dear to myself may be worthless in the eyes of those to whom my papers fall.' The answer came from the same source that had long inspired his love of reading about the early saints, their lives largely revealed in correspondence. When he wrote about St John Chrysostom, he showed that he was attracted by his humanity, by the revelation in his correspondence and other writings of a moral identity with its growth and continuity, the inward life of one individual character. Consistently with this, he believed that the best biography would be made from the letters of the subject: when he realized that some day his biography would be written he composed a third person memoir of the years up to 1830 and handed over the memoir and his letters written as an Anglican, along with letters to him, to his sister-in-law Anne Mozley. One of the reasons she was chosen was because he was sure they should have an Anglican editor. A reading of Newman's books, memoranda and letters disabuses one further of the idea that self-consciousness is identical with self-absorption. When he wrote a letter or a sermon or a book, he was always deeply conscious of and concerned with his reader or hearer. Co-extensive with the luminous self-evidence of his own being was a consciousness of the mystery of external reality. As a child, he recorded: 'I thought Life might be a dream, or I an Angel, and all this world a deception, my fellow-Angels by a playful device concealing themselves from me, and deceiving me with the semblance of a material world.'[4]

Newman did not care for 'paper logic': the 'whole man' was central for him. That reflects his own fully rounded nature: all his endowments, physical, mental, spiritual, were seen as good and developed, although some things good in themselves had to be subordinated to the greater good. Newman's 'whole man' was developed at Oxford and continued flowering at the Oratory, where he lived a hidden life. It had its root in his family and upbringing, and the early soil which nourished them was that of a special domestic happiness. We catch glimpses of the mature Newman in the little boy. One anecdote of his sister Jemima's will have to suffice here:

> After an infantile struggle for mastery between mother and son – the loving mother and her strong-willed child – she reminded him, 'You see, John, you did not get your own way.' 'No,' was his answer, 'but I tried very hard.'[5]

His healthy constitution brought him through a severe fever in Sicily when he was 32. Although never a games player, he was a tireless walker and rider, who as a young man enjoyed the exhilaration of jumping on horseback; he never learned to swim, but he took to the cold plunge as a child in pools and streams, and as an

27

elderly man he continued to take a cold shower. Another physical characteristic and one expressive of his inner self was a low sweet musical speaking voice, not loud but clear; Matthew Arnold in memorable words wrote of its contribution to the powerful effect of his sermons in St Mary's; and most of the old friends, from whom he had been separated for years by his conversion, when they met him again mentioned the survival of his beautiful voice into old age. His firm will carried him through the difficulties of life. It served him above all in making his life comfortable to the intentions of God for him. Even after the enthusiasm of youth was over, he continued to labour while it was yet day. That required will. Newman was an omnivorous reader all his life, with novels providing a happy recreation. Among contemporary novelists his favourites in middle and old age were Thackeray and Trollope. He told the friend who gave him *Barchester Towers*, his first Trollope, that after beginning it he woke himself out of his night's sleep, laughing at the memory.

Newman also had a deep love of music, to which he was introduced at home. His father gave him a violin when he was ten and provided him with a teacher. The composer who meant most to him was Beethoven, who he once said was like 'a great bird singing'.

His happy family, relaxed school, and university helped him gain extensive knowledge and to reflect on what he knew; they were also ideal environments for someone with a gift for friendship. In one of his sets of verses he wrote of the 'blessing of friends that to my door unasked, unsought have come';[6] the words express his appreciation of the value of friends and his innate modesty – they had made him a gift that he could not have solicited. His were not only strong but constant feelings: he never lost a friend from schooldays onwards; though as time went on he was parted from them by death – but the dates were written in a notebook and remembered in his prayers every year. Perhaps the most rewarding of these relationships was the friendship of equals with his contemporary Hurrell Froude; less intellectual than Newman and drawn to the Church of the Middle Ages rather than the Fathers, but able to share with him ideas – and jokes; they worked together to reform the Oriel tutorial system until Hawkins, the new Provost, put a stop to it. His premature death from consumption in 1836 was a deep sadness.

It was his capacity for friendship that made him so fit to be an

Oratorian. Wiseman had suggested it, and while in Italy Newman observed and was instantly drawn to the Roman Community at the Chiesa Nuova. 'It is like a college with hardly any rule. They keep their own property and furnish their own rooms.'[7] It was at Birmingham that he founded his own Oratory and it was at Birmingham that the quarrel with Faber was born which was to lead to the separate foundation of the London Oratory. Relations between the two Oratories varied from the openly hostile to the deeply suspicious, and they remain divided to this day. Newman would have appreciated the irony embodied in his statue in Knightsbridge, erected after his death, and which has caused many people to think of the London Oratory as Newman's home. Whatever it was, it was never that – Newman's *nido* was not in fashionable Brompton but in a Birmingham suburb.

If Newman had friends he also had enemies. Faber was a shadow on Newman's life until Faber died. He is accurately described as an 'enemy', but Newman visited him before his death, gave him his blessing and commended him to St Philip Neri. Yet his verdict on Faber did not change; it was that 'with many shining, many winning qualities, he has no heart'. In 1865, after the deaths of Faber and Cardinal Wiseman, he wrote in his journal: 'The two chief persons, whom I felt to be unjust to me are gone – the Cardinal and Faber. Their place has been taken by Manning and Ward; but somehow from my never having been brought into close contact with either of them, as with the Cardinal and Faber, I have not that sense of their cruelty which I felt so much as regards the two last mentioned.'[8] Cardinal Manning and W G Ward, especially the Cardinal, were certainly enemies; they were responsible for preventing his return to Oxford to set up an Oratory there (advanced as far as buying the land), and he was almost deprived of his Cardinalate by Manning's jealous intervention.

Newman's strong family feeling and affectionate nature might have been expected to lead to marriage. Neither accidental circumstances nor temperament prevented him. From boyhood his young sisters were close companions, as their charming and amusing letters to each other show; the sudden death of his merry youngest sister, Mary, was a deep grief and she was never forgotten. Through his relations and his Oxford friends he met, and enjoyed the company of, women; and they enjoyed his. He loved and was at his ease with children – as one might expect from the eldest son in a happy family and a man who retained contact with his own childhood self. As a young man he can be found with friends' children on his knee, pulling his glasses on and off and chattering to him. In old age his child friends included R W Church's little daughters. Helen gave him *Alice in Wonderland*, which he enjoyed, and then the *Hunting of the Snark*: Newman said that it reminded him of his own thoughts and feelings as a small boy, when 'I lay in my crib in the early spring, with outdoor scents, sounds and sights wakening me up, and especially the cheerful ring of the mower's scythe on the lawn'.[9] His celibacy was deliberately chosen and the result of a gradual development. In the *Apologia* this reticent man says that he is 'obliged to mention', reluctantly, the 'deep imagination' which took possession of him in the autumn of 1816, the time when he experienced inward conversion, which he identified as 'the beginning of divine faith in me'. That deep imagination, he wrote, was 'that it would be the will of God that I should lead a single life'. 'This anticipation, which has held its ground almost continuously ever since – with the break of a month now and a month then, up to 1829, and after that date, without any break at all – was more or less connected, in my mind, with the notion that my calling in life would require such a sacrifice as celibacy involved.'[10] By 1829 Hurrell Froude had introduced him to the positive ideal of virginity; as Newman said, 'He had a high severe idea of the intrinsic excellence of Virginity; and he considered the Blessed Virgin as its great pattern.'[11] Newman's resolution involved no depreciation of marriage; in his thirties he acknowledged his lack of the sympathy that only a wife could give and regretted that he would not have children.

There is a holiness of places as well as of persons. Newman always felt the deep solace and inspiration drawn from loved places and beautiful landscape. He had what Bagehot described as the one thing necessary for a great experience – an experiencing nature. The family's country retreat at Ham, given up when he was six, had been how he visualized heaven as a child, and more than fifty years later, on revisiting the place he said that he could still 'have passed an examination in it'. In May 1828, after the death of his sister Mary, he wrote to his sister Jemima about a ride to Cuddesdon:

The country, too, is beautiful; the fresh leaves, the scents, the varied landscape. Yet I never felt so intensely the transitory nature of this world as when most delighted with these country scenes . . . I wish it were possible for words to put down those indefinite, vague, and withal subtle feelings which quite pierce the soul and make it sick. Dear Mary seems embodied in every tree and hid behind every hill. What a veil and curtain this world of sense is! beautiful, but still a veil.[12]

The idea of a greater reality hidden by human circumstance was included in the words he chose for his gravestone: *Ex umbris et imaginibus in veritatem* (from shades and images into truth). His keen sense of nature's varied beauty never failed. He had an impressionist feeling for light and colour; he had also a sense of form and once said that a great bare open prospect meant most to him. When in 1831 he stayed with the Froudes at Dartington, he was overcome by the Devon landscape – although he found the 'exuberance of the grass and foliage oppressive, as if one had not room to breathe'. To his mother he wrote:

What strikes me most is the strange richness of everything. The rocks blush into every variety of colour, the trees and fields are emeralds, and the cottages are rubies. A beetle I picked up at Torquay was as green and gold as the stone it lay upon, and a squirrel which ran up a tree here just now was not the pale reddish-brown to which I am accustomed, but a bright brown-red. Nay, my very hands and fingers look rosy, like Homer's Aurora, and I have been gazing on them with astonishment . . . The scents are extremely fine, so very delicate yet so powerful, and the colours of the flowers as if they were all shot with white. The sweet peas especially have the complexion of a beautiful face. They trail up the wall mixed with myrtles as creepers. As to the sunset, the Dartmoor heights look purple, and the sky close upon them a clear orange.[13]

The landscape to which he attached most significance was that of Sicily. In 1833 on his first journey abroad, accompanying Hurrell Froude and Hurrell's father, he was seized with a desire to see Sicily and exerted his strong will to cross alone from the Italian mainland while his friends returned home. There he caught a fever, lasting three weeks, when he was close to death but saved by his strong constitution, the tender care of the Italian guide he had hired, and the kindness of the family with whom they lodged. Before he fell ill

31

he experienced an ecstatic pleasure in the scenery, conveyed in one of his letters to his mother and sisters:

> The two last miles we diverged from the road up a steep path, and soon came to the ancient stone ascent leading up to Taurominium. I never saw anything more enchanting than this spot. It realised all that one had read of it in books about the scenery – a deep valley, brawling streams, beautiful trees, the sea (heard) in the distance. But when, after breakfast, on a bright day we mounted to the theatre, and saw the famous view, what shall I say? I never knew that Nature could be so beautiful; and to see that view was the nearest approach to seeing Eden. O happy I! It was worth coming all the way, to endure sadness, loneliness, weariness, to see it. I felt, for the first time in my life that I should be a better and more religious man if I lived there.[14]

He returned to England, after recovery from the fever, almost unrecognizable from its effects, including the temporary loss of his thick brown hair. Despite this, he was full of even more than his usual joyous energy, physical, mental and spiritual: he might have said, as he did in 1826, 'I could have rooted up St Mary's spire and kicked down the Radcliffe.'

The French have crystallized a truth that the English have sometimes forgotten – 'Style is the Man'. Of no one is it more true than of Newman. He was a writer of genius and his style is the salt which has preserved his thoughts and feelings for the century since his death. As a child he wrote to his family, kept a diary, produced plays and verses; as a youth he made personal memoranda, influenced stylistically by Gibbon and Hume, since he began – as many writers do – by imitation. When destroying some of his early writings, he said: 'I seldom wrote without an eye to style and since my taste was bad, my style was bad. I wrote in style as another might write in verse, or sing instead of speaking, or dance instead of walking.'[15] From his mid twenties onwards his essays and memoranda show an individual and increasingly flexible style, which blossomed in his first full-length book, *The Arians*. His sermons changed too: he was conscious of the moment when the change crystallized, on one of his long walks in 1827. He suddenly saw that a series of numbered points was not the way to reach his congregation, but the concentration on, and expansion of, one thought. He was supreme as a prose writer. Take what is sometimes called Cardinal Newman's Prayer:

> May he support us all the day long, till the shades lengthen, and the evening comes, and the busy world is hushed, and the fever of life is over and our work is done. Then in his mercy may he give us a safe lodging and a holy rest and peace at the last.

This is not in fact a special prayer but the ending of one of his ordinary sermons.[16] From childhood he had thrown off verses, finding that process a recreation which made fewer demands than prose – he was capable of verse even while suffering from sea-sickness, as he discovered on his journey abroad in 1833. He was the main contributor of verses printed in the *British Magazine* to spread and reinforce the principles opposed to 'Liberalism' in the Church. His and the other contributions were collected in the *Lyra Apostolica*, which Bagehot took with him on his honeymoon. One, intensely personal, has been preserved by its use as a hymn, the untitled poem whose first line is, 'Lead kindly Light, amid the encircling gloom'. He continued to write verse, and his most powerful poem, *The Dream of Gerontius*, dating from 1865, on death and the soul and the grace of God, is known to thousands, thanks to a felicitous combination with Elgar's splendid music. But writing his great prose was not a recreation nor an inspired outpouring. Newman, like Pope, laboured to communicate precisely *and* to give aesthetic pleasure. There was also something of the eighteenth century in his modest, well-mannered insistence on the 'occasional' nature of his writing, on never – except for the *Grammar of Assent* – writing without a call. Yet many a call need not have been heard, except by a born writer's ear. He more than once said in his memoranda that the process of writing brought out his thought more clearly to himself; a good quill pen, good ink, were important; he wrote in a well-formed flowing handwriting and when age slowed its speed he found his thoughts moved more slowly.

Newman's writings, and through them the author's personality, move the heart. As he wrote in his brilliant and excoriating attack on Brougham and Peel, *The Tamworth Reading Room*: 'The heart is commonly reached, not through the reason, but through the imagination, by means of direct impressions, by the testimony of facts and events, by history, by description.'[17] And he went on in a sentence copied out by Matthew Arnold in his *Notebooks* on three separate occasions: 'Persons influence us, voices melt us, looks subdue us, deeds inflame us.' Miscellaneous useful knowledge could neither heal nor educate. That could only be done by a reality, incarnate in words, that is found in every part of his manifold writings.

Cor ad cor loquitur ('Heart speaks to heart'): such was the motto which he chose as cardinal. Heart indeed speaks to heart. The writings, which are those of a 'whole man' for whom religion was 'real', move today as surely as the day on which they were written. They have a universal appeal.

NOTES

1. 'Autobiographical Memoir' of 1874 in *John Henry Newman: Autobiographical Writings*, ed. H Tristram (Sheed & Ward 1956), p. 30.
2. ibid., p. 63.
3. *Letters & Diaries of John Henry Newman*, ed. C S Dessain et al. (Oxford, Clarendon Press, 1961–84), vol. xi., p. 132. The letter was to W J Copeland. (*Letters & Diaries* henceforth abbreviated as LD.)
4. *Apologia*, p. 1.
5. *Letters & Correspondence of John Henry Newman during his Life in the English Church*, ed. Anne Mozley (London 1891), vol. i, p. 16.
6. *Verses on Various Occasions* (Longmans 1889), no. xv, 'A Thanksgiving' (written 20th Oct. 1829).
7. LD, xi, 305 (31st Dec. 1846 to J D Dalgairns).
8. 'The Journal' (1859–79) in op. cit., ed. H Tristram (entry for 22 Feb. 1865), p. 260.
9. LD, xxviii, 52 (to Helen Church, 19th April 1876).
10. *Apologia* (Sheed & Ward 1976), p. 5.
11. ibid., p. 16. But for a rather different account of the development of Newman's devotion to the Virgin Mary, cf. F W Newman, *The Early History of Cardinal Newman*, pp. 18–24.
12. LD, ii, 69 (10th May 1828).
13. ibid., ii, 343 (7th July 1831).
14. ibid., iii, 303 (25th April 1833).
15. In op. cit., ed. H Tristram, p. 149 (introduction to 'Early Journals: Book I').
16. 'Wisdom and Innocence', in *Sermons on Subjects of the Day* (Rivingtons 1885) no. xx, p. 307 (first preached 19th Feb. 1843).
17. *Tamworth Reading Room*, letter 6; repeated in *Grammar of Assent*, ch. 4, sec. 3.

· 2 ·

Newman and Oxford

DAVID NEWSOME

Newman was an undergraduate at Trinity College from 1817 to 1820 and a Fellow of Oriel between 1822 and 1845 when his conversion to Roman Catholicism required him to resign his fellowship. The rules at Oxford changed gradually thereafter, first with undergraduate degrees being thrown open to those of any religion or none in 1854 and then teaching fellowships in 1871. It was the latter move which made possible Newman's election to an honorary fellowship at Trinity in 1877. Thus while Newman remained at Oxford it had been exclusively Anglican, though he had tried hard to change the character of that Anglicanism by the leading role he had played in the reforming group that came to be known as the Oxford Movement. One of the leading historians in England of that movement is Dr David Newsome. There could therefore scarcely be a better choice of person to answer the question: What was the influence of Oxford upon him?

It must be accounted a very great privilege for a Cambridge man to be invited to Oxford to contribute to this series of lectures in honour of John Henry Newman's centenary, the more so since the subject on which I have been asked to comment is the most intimately Oxonian of all – the relationship between Newman and the university which successively reared him, feared him and (in the end) revered him – 'Newman and Oxford': a great man and a great seat of learning so closely linked in the judgement of posterity that it is almost true to say that Oxford would never have been quite the same without him, as it is indisputably true to say that Newman could not have been Newman had he been educated elsewhere. It

35

was all the doing of the curate of St James's Piccadilly, a Mr John Mullens, a man of no historical consequence save for the circumstance that he happened to be passing the door of the Newman household, where the post-chaise was waiting, with the fifteen-year old John Henry sitting somewhat apprehensively inside, while his father debated whether to instruct the coachman to take the road to Cambridge or to Oxford; and the good Mr Mullens, who happened to be a graduate of Exeter College and an acquaintance of Mr Newman, offered to accompany them to Oxford there and then.

Let us change the scene to Cambridge for a moment. In 1882, Matthew Arnold delivered the Rede Lecture of that year, and ventured to compare the two great universities. 'The University of Oxford', he said, 'has produced great men, indeed, but has above all been the source or the centre of great movements . . . within the range of what is called modern history . . . . We have the great movements of Royalism, Wesleyanism, Tractarianism, Ritualism. . . . You have nothing of the kind . . . . Yours is a University not of great movements', but he did have the graciousness to concede that Cambridge had produced its fair share of great men.[1] Perhaps I have slightly overstated the note of implicit condescension from the lips of that Oxford savant, to whom condescension came rather easily, but there is an element of truth in what he said. It is open to doubt, indeed, whether Newman, had he taken that road to Cambridge, would have become a great man at all. Would he ever have grown out of his youthful Calvinist Evangelicalism if nurtured in the fertile soil of the university of Charles Simeon – and what would have been the consequence of that, in the history of the Anglican and Roman Churches? The Newman that the world knows was fashioned by the University of Oxford, through the particular intellectual influences that he encountered in his formative years there at a particularly stimulating phase of Oxford's history; it was Oxford that both inspired him with a cause and endowed him with the confidence to prosecute it. Moreover – and make of this what you will – in Newman's own words, speaking of himself and his fellow-converts, 'Oxford made us Catholics'.[2] Of such strange twists of fate, history abounds.

Certainly no one who knew the shy and timid young Trinity undergraduate of those first few years could have foreseen what the future would hold in store. He felt utterly out of his depth, self-conscious about his lack of years as well as his lack of poise and, to some extent, his lack of the classical training enjoyed by the products of public schools. He was horrified by the drinking propensities of his companions, especially the wealthier sort, and, indeed, he was no more enamoured of the arrogance and dissipation of the gentlemen-commoners of Oriel, when he became Fellow and Tutor there. He was by nature solitary, and in this respect he never changed. He fed, almost greedily, upon the companionship of a single soul-mate – John Bowden at Trinity, then Hurrell Froude (until his early death) at Oriel – and never felt at ease in company. No wonder that he was overawed by the brilliant and disputatious Oriel Senior Common Room when he became a Fellow in 1822. He was either tongue-tied in their company or, when socializing was unavoidable, somewhat facetious and jejune, a trait which Maisie Ward has noted as persisting until about the age of 26.[3] All this, together with his collapse through over-work in the Schools, resulting in a lowly degree, makes it the more surprising that Oriel took the risk, knowing that it was a risk, of electing him to the coveted prize Fellowship. Perhaps he was a bit lucky, too. Had he deferred his attempt on the Fellowship examination to a year later, he would have been competing against E B Pusey and Edward Churton.

It is to Oriel's credit that Newman prospered both intellectually and in terms of his growth in self-confidence. During the period between 1822 and 1830 he encountered, with varying degrees of intimacy, those who were to become his mentors: Richard Whately, Joseph Blanco White and Edward Hawkins. It was Hawkins who began the process of weaning Newman from his Evangelical sympathies into an understanding of the centrality of baptismal regeneration and the role of the *ecclesia docens* (The 'teaching church') – an exercise in the appreciation of the Catholic and apostolic traditions of the Anglican Church completed by the greatest influence of all, that of John Keble. Newman was to acknowledge these influences in the *Apologia* many years later, even though his friendship with each of them, Keble alone excepted, was to be severed, not without bitterness on either side.

The transformation in Newman over these years was threefold. In the first place, he discovered the abiding source of inspiration for his understanding of Christian doctrine, the sacramental principle and the role of the teaching Church through his study of the Fathers, leading him to the conclusion, as he put it in the *Apologia*, that 'Antiquity was the true exponent of the doctrines of Christianity and the basis of the Church of England'.[4] His close association with John Keble over this period would have acquainted him with the Anglican tradition of patristic veneration in the writings of the Caroline divines, although – according to Dr T M Parker[5] – Newman's serious reading of writers like Laud, Bramhall and Stillingfleet was very much a postscript to his study of the Fathers and largely due to the influence of that rare example of a traditional High Churchman among the Oxford Heads of Houses, Dr Martin Routh, President of Magdalen College. With this background, supported and stimulated by the compelling spirituality and humility of Keble, the ardent romanticism of Hurrell Froude and the more sober scholarship of Edward Pusey, Newman's churchmanship within the Catholic, apostolic, sacramental and ecclesiological tradition was soon firmly set.

But two other transformations, equally the product of Oxford, are worthy of note. Newman emerged from his shell. There are a number of reasons why. Whately had faithfully and successfully discharged his commission of drawing him out and knocking him into shape; he had been given College office as a Tutor (also, rather improbably, College Cellarer); he had acquired an absorbing cure of souls as Vicar of St Mary's in 1828; he had gathered around him some like-minded friends; but above all, he had discovered a cause – the determination to prevent Sir Robert Peel's re-election as Member for Oxford in 1829, following his *volte-face* on the issue of Catholic Emancipation. In retrospect, this was rather a sorry business, one cannot but feel. Quite apart from the irony of Newman's first demonstration of militancy being aimed at perpetuating the deprivations of his future co-religionists, his intemperate language, although not untypical of an angry young man, especially a *shy* angry young man who has for the first time discovered the thrill of battle and the satisfaction of being on the winning side, was extravagant and unpleasing, to say the least. To describe Sir Robert Peel as a 'rat', or to declare that it was 'better to be bigotted than time-serving'[6] certainly did not endear him to those who had striven so hard on his behalf in earlier years, Whately and Hawkins, and the severance of these friendships was to have an unhappy sequel. Newman crowed with triumph when Peel was defeated. 'We have achieved a glorious Victory. It is the first public event I have been concerned in, and I thank God from my heart both for my cause and its success. We have proved the independence of the Church and of Oxford.'[7] The Oxford Movement, traditionally dated from the Assize Sermon of John Keble in 1833, had to all intents and purposes begun.

Oxford, then, endowed Newman with a particular brand of churchmanship, both a cause to fight for and the increasing confidence to join battle. More than that, however, it sharpened the weapons that he was time and time again to employ. I don't think that Oxford taught Newman his incomparable *style*; that was more a combination of Cicero, Gibbon, a natural poetic sense and a musical ear. But it taught him the Aristotelian *method*. I have argued elsewhere that Newman was by nature a Platonist. Was there ever anything so thoroughly Platonic as his earliest world-picture, in which he conceived 'life to be a dream, or I an Angel, and all this world a deception'?[8] What Oxford achieved, partly through its curriculum in the Schools and partly through the notorious 'logic-chopping' of the Oriel Common Room, where vestiges of the earlier Noeticism survived, was to graft a strong and virile Aristotelian, empiricist, shoot on to that fundamentally Platonic, idealist stock. They could not change Newman's temperament, however, or his philosophical disposition. As soon as Newman encountered the Alexandrian Fathers, he was at home again in the world of universals, forms and symbols. But he never lost the logical and rhetorical arts which a sound training in Aristotle can foster in a highly receptive mind. Let an Oxford man, G M Young, describe it:

> Often when I am reading Newman, an unholy analogy presents itself, and, as he would have said, 'stains my imagination'. I cannot help thinking of those African virgins who in Gibbon's language 'admitted priests and deacons to their bed, and gloried amidst the flames in their unsullied purity'. He is always skimming along the verge of a logical catastrophe, and always relying on his dialectic agility to save himself from falling; always exposing what seems to be an unguarded spot, and always revealing a new line of defence when the unwary assailant has reached it. I am not sure it is not a general characteristic of Oxford: we are not the children of Ockham for nothing; and we are all, I think, more ready to take intellectual risks than they are at 'the less ancient and splendid place', trusting to Aristotle to

inspire us with the right mood and figure when needed, and so to preserve 'the unsullied purity' of our reasoning.[9]

We are now, however, entering that period of Newman's life which he described as 'the time of plenty'[10] the fifteen years between 1828 and 1843, coinciding with his incumbency of the University Church, St Mary's. During 1830, he had – not from his own choice – effectively turned his back on Oriel, as the result of his conflict with the new Provost, Edward Hawkins, over his concept of the role of a college tutor, shared by his two fellow-tutors, Robert Wilberforce and Hurrell Froude. Keble had been Newman's inspiration here, regarding a tutorship as an office primarily of pastoral care. After all, were it otherwise, Keble had commented, a clergyman had no call to abandon a cure of souls to take on such a post.[11] This was exactly how Newman and his two colleagues conceived it. Hawkins, however, thought otherwise. He objected to the principle of discrimination whereby tutors could devote their attention to the abler men, leaving the idler gentlemen-commoners very much to their own devices while a special pastoral relationship was created between each tutor and his favoured few. It was an issue on which there was an element of right on both sides; but since neither party was prepared to give way, Hawkins effectively dismissed the three tutors by refusing to allocate pupils to them. Keble, when he heard the news, thought that Hawkins had gone out of his mind. He was certainly high-handed. But perhaps Mark Pattison's later judgement was more perceptive. Hawkins had taken a step that would lead to a decline in the quality of Oriel men; on the other hand, if Newman had had his way, Oriel could well have turned into a sort of seminary.[12]

Alas, neither of the two men was prepared to forgive and forget. Years later, in 1877, when Trinity invited Newman to become the College's first honorary fellow, Newman declared where his heart lay. His affection for Trinity was 'greater than for any thing in Oxford'. While he had had 'more, and more intimately personal, Oriel friends . . . there was too much painful at Oriel . . . hence I rejoice that it is Trinity, not Oriel, that has reclaimed me.'[13] Immediately, however, the loss of the tutorship meant that Newman could give his full attention to other things. There was his parish, and his patristic studies; and, as soon as he had returned from his Mediterranean tour with Froude, followed by his illness in Sicily, on the one hand so physically shattered that he lost his hair and had to wear a wig, and, on the other, in the belligerent mood of Achilles returning to the fray, there was seemingly the greatest cause in his life to respond to: the defence of 'the Church in danger'. This was the battle cry of the High Church party at the determination of the Whigs in 1833 to reform the scandalously unreformed Irish Church. Their initial *riposte* was the launching of the Tracts for the Times.

Years later, trying to recapture the atmosphere of Oxford during the following stormy, yet exhilarating, decade, Benjamin Jowett reflected to Wilfrid Ward, 'it was the age of young men'.[14] Well, every age, I suppose, is that; but some ages perhaps more so than others. This was the period when the Romantic Movement was at its height, with its ardent faith in individualism on the one hand, and on the other its susceptibility to all that spoke of the mysterious, the irrational and the arcane; this was a time, too, of tumultuous change – both actual, in the acceleration of the pace of life with the advent of the railways, and potential, with the fear of violent social upheaval as the barricades were set up yet again in the streets of Paris. If an eager response to the call for order, stability, discipline and the insights of ages long past were to be found anywhere, it would surely come from that traditional bastion of orthodoxy, Oxford. Equally certain, however, was it that belligerence would beget belligerence. For the real enemy of Tractarianism was Liberalism, and the anti-dogmatic latitudinarianism of Arnold, Whately and the Noetics.

Dr Johnson once observed that the ancient Greeks could argue good-humouredly about religion because they did not believe in it. Officially, at least, there could be no such thing as an unbeliever at Oxford because it was impossible to be admitted to the University without subscription to the Thirty-Nine Articles; and the fellowship body of every college was exclusively clerical. The conflict, therefore, was bound to be intense and acrimonious. From the Tractarian side it was conducted on two fronts – in the publication of the widely-circulated Tracts, and through what Wilfrid Ward described as 'the slender instruments'[15] of Newman's personal influence as Vicar of St Mary's, his Sunday evening sermons and the occasional lectures that he delivered in the Adam de Brome chapel. What started as a cause became a sort of crusade, and Oxford, as the party divisions hardened, took upon itself the aspect and ethos of a late-medieval city-state (according to Dean Church) wherein strife became the more bitter and rivalries and devotions more intense within the parochialism of a close-knit community.[16] Here was a Regius Professor deprived of his right to vote for Select Preachers because suspicions of heresy had been aroused in a book so dull that very few had actually read it, and those that had maintained that it was unintelligible. There were tales of Heads of Houses and Doctors of Divinity paying clandestine visits to Littlemore, where they took refuge behind a hedge to spy on alleged monastic goings-on. Scandalized delight was exhibited when the news got abroad that Thomas Arnold, Headmaster of Rugby, allowed his teenage children to undress together in the same room and that the whole family would then indulge in mixed bathing. No wonder that he held unsound views about the nature of the Established Church.[17] The world, of course, has changed. Oxford is no longer clerical Oxford; and one has to concede that the young of today, in contrast to those undergraduates of the 1830s who flocked to Newman's pulpit at St Mary's, would doubtless find the evocations of the heroic age of the early saints and martyrs fractionally less beguiling.

Although Newman never set out to beguile, and always imposed upon himself the greatest restraint as a preacher, the memory of his remarkable addresses lingered for a lifetime. Gladstone, in 1879 at a dinner-party, observed to his fellow-guests that he saw the beginning of the Newman cult, just before he went down in 1832. It had already become the custom 'to go and hear him on Sunday afternoons'. 'I do not believe', he said, 'that there has been anything like his influence in Oxford, when it was at its height, since Abelard lectured in Paris.'[18] As late as 1883, Matthew Arnold in his lecture on 'Emerson', looked back to those golden days. 'I seem to hear him still', he said, recalling vividly a sermon that he had never actually heard.[19]

Matthew Arnold may be forgiven. He undoubtedly did witness Newman preaching. He would have read Newman's sermons later, because so many of them were published. It has to be remembered that Newman was writing prolifically during this period, producing unquestionably his most creative work. These were the years of the *Parochial and Plain Sermons* (which Gladstone maintained would prove to be the most enduring of all his writings)[20] and of twenty-seven (actually twenty-seven and a half) contributions to the *Tracts for the Times*; they were the years also of *The Arians of the Fourth Century* and of his two attempts to expound the nature of

Anglicanism as the *via media* between Roman Catholicism and popular Protestantism, in the *Prophetical Office* and the *Lectures on Justification*. Both his *Oxford University Sermons* and the superb essay on the Tamworth Reading-Room are anticipations of things to come, because the standpoint and arguments of both reappear, in their classical expression, in *The Idea of a University* and *A Grammar of Assent*. Finally, although admittedly written on his Anglican deathbed, came *An Essay on the Development of Christian Doctrine*. Practically every one of Newman's original and characteristic insights in the realms of theology, philosophy and educational theory can be traced back to the last ten years of his Oxford career.

Conflict there was bound to be. When Newman declared that it was 'Oxford who made us Catholics' his intention seems to have been to acknowledge his debt to his Oxford study of the Fathers and the way in which this eventually led to his conversion. But we may also legitimately ask the question of the events of the time: did Oxford force him to become a Catholic? Were he and others driven from the Church of their baptism by an unholy alliance at Oxford between the forces of liberalism and evangelicalism which eventually provoked the Establishment (the episcopal bench and the Oxford Heads of Houses) to condemn the attempt to define the Catholic and apostolic nature of Anglicanism? Newman had certainly made powerful enemies in Oxford: C P Golightly for one, a former Oriel pupil, whom Newman had invited to be his curate at Littlemore, only subsequently to withdraw the invitation on discovering a difference of views over baptismal regeneration; Godfrey Faussett, the Lady Margaret Professor of Divinity; Edward Hawkins, as we have already noted. To some extent Newman needlessly, even mischievously, provoked his opponents, although his private opinion of Golightly ('a goose') and Faussett ('an old macaw') may not have reached their ears.[21] The ill-advised publication of Froude's *Remains* in the opening months of 1838 was the moment when the authorities began to take fright. Newman's act of devotion to a dear friend, following his untimely death, was taken as a declaration of war by those appalled at Froude's unconcealed admiration for the Roman Church and his contemptuous treatment of the Reformers. The question was bound to be raised – how could such sentiments accord with subscription to the Thirty-Nine Articles? Newman's answer to this was the notoriously controversial Tract 90. Newman said subsequently that the attack on this tract, culminating in the 'Protest of the Four Tutors' and the condemnation by the Hebdomadal Board, arose from the fact that 'an essay written for one set of people' was 'read and misunderstood by another set'.[22] What he meant was that the tract was intended to exhibit to the younger and more extreme adherents of the Tractarian cause that the Thirty-Nine Articles 'might be interpreted, and subscribed, in a sense compatible with the faith of the ancient church',[23] but that his adversaries seized upon it as confirmation of his pro-Roman sympathies and therefore his insidious influence upon under-graduates. It was undoubtedly naive of Newman not to have foreseen the consequences. He could, perhaps, have shrugged off the 'Cry Havoc' from the powers-that-be at Oxford; unfortunately, however, they let slip those improbable dogs of war – the episcopal bench.

This presented Newman with an insoluble dilemma. For him, the bishop was 'his Pope' – the voice of apostolic authority which the Anglican Church had to possess if it were a true *ecclesia docens*. The various hostile Charges of the bishops were, to him, a desperate rebuff, emanating from the very people whose authority he had done so much to enhance. F L Cross put forward the view, some fifty years ago, that this rebuff was decisive in compelling Newman to turn to Rome as a sort of 'psychological retaliation' against the Church which had rejected him.[24] It led him to resign the living of St Mary's, certainly; but his decision to become a Roman Catholic was a positive, not a negative, step. His reappraisal of the early centuries of the Christian Church led him sincerely to believe the Anglican Church to be in schism, so that he was fearful for the safety of his own soul. So we return to his statement that 'Oxford made us Catholics'. It was at Oxford that Newman discovered the Fathers; and, as he observed in his published letter to Pusey's *Eirenicon* of 1864, 'The Fathers made me a Catholic, and I am not going to knock down the ladder by which I ascended into the Church.'[25]

So Newman and Oxford parted company in the year 1845, and they were not to see each other again for thirty-two years. Ten years earlier, in June 1867, Newman paid a sentimental journey to Littlemore in the company of Ambrose St John. There is also a curious episode recounted in the unpublished journals of Stopford Brooke of what I can only describe as a 'sighting' of Newman (because it is not recorded elsewhere), which is, alas, undated. It is

so extraordinary – and, indeed, so little known – that I offer it to
you now:

> Monday, 24 January 1898: [Mr Barrow] told an interesting tale of
> Card[inal] Newman . . . One day Barrow was in the room under
> the library at Oriel, when the door opened, and in came an old,
> greyheaded man, walking infirmly – whom he recognised to his
> wonder as Newman. He went to the table, pulled out the drawers
> and seemed looking for something. At last, he came up to Barrow
> – 'Can you tell me where the key of the library is. It used to be in
> this drawer?' 'It is not there now', said Barrow, 'the books were
> taken away and it was put into my charge.' Then Newman smiled
> and said, 'Thirty years ago I took a book home from the library,
> and I have never been able to remember whether I put it back or
> not. I had to leave Oxford suddenly. I have looked for it at home. I
> cannot find it – and now, being in Oxford again for the first time,
> I want to see whether it is in the library. I should like to settle my
> conscience about it. I have thought of it all these years.'
>
> So Barrow gave him the key, and the old man went upstairs
> and remained for half an hour. 'I could not find it', he said when
> he came down, and he went away. That visit is not mentioned in
> his life. I liked the story. It belonged to the man. I wonder what he
> thought of in that silent half hour and in that ugly room. I may
> fancy it, but I may not say it.[26]

What was the effect upon Oxford of his going? In the opinion of
some it settled down to a saner and steadier pace of life. Mark
Pattison, in his *Memoirs*, noted:

> a sudden lull which fell upon Oxford . . . the moment the
> secessions to Rome were announced . . . We felt old things had
> passed away, but by no means that all things had become new.
> Common conversation seemed to have collapsed, to have died out
> for want of topic. The railway mania of 1847 and King Hudson
> was the first material that rushed in to fill up the vacuum.

Then came the revolutions of 1848.

> It seemed incredible, in the presence of such an upheaval, that we
> had been spending years in debating any matter so flimsy as
> whether England was in a state of schism or no . . . The truth is
> that this moment, which swept the leader of the Tractarians, with

most of his followers out of the place, was an epoch in the history of the University. It was a deliverance from the nightmare which had oppressed Oxford for fifteen years.[27]

This is a characteristic, hard-bitten Pattisonian sentiment. It was confirmed, however, in less emotive language, at least in part, by the Royal Commission of 1852. Two years later, Matthew Arnold commented on the apathetic mood in Oxford at that time, comparing it unfavourably with Paris, Germany and even London. 'Animation and interest and the power of work seem so sadly wanting . . . The place, in losing Newman, and his followers, has lost its religious movement, which after all kept it from stagnating, and has not yet, so far as I can see, got anything better.'[28]

And what of Newman? He missed his Oxford friends greatly. He had no one now to talk with, unlike the old Oriel days, he remarked to Mrs Bowden in 1849,[29] 'All my human affections were with those whom I had left', he told Manning glumly in 1861.[30] Manning would have understood this, because he shared the sentiment. In his old age, he befriended the much younger Oxonian, J E C Bodley, whom he first met when serving on the Housing Commission. Often Bodley would visit Manning, late in the evening, at the 'grim barrack called Archbishop's House' (once described by Shane Leslie as resembling 'a Dissenting chapel doing duty as a railway waiting room'),[31] and on these occasions the Cardinal would look back to his Oxford days. Alighting on a copy of the *Scholar Gipsy*, Manning once observed to Bodley, 'Ah! Only Oxford men like you and me can understand that . . . Only Oxford men like us . . . Nobody here understands Oxford; none of them have quite understood me.'[32]

Of course Newman felt lonely; but however much he missed that happier 'time of plenty', he could still say to Pusey, in a letter written in 1866, when the question of the founding of an Oratory Mission in Oxford had been first mooted, 'Oxford can never be to me what it was. It and I are severed, it would be like the dead visiting the dead. I should be a stranger in my dearest home.'[33] Nevertheless, both the idea and the ideal of Oxford haunted Newman throughout his Catholic career. The rule of St Philip Neri and the style of the Oratory life – a community of like-minded men 'dedicated to religious work, learned studies, literary pursuits and the fine arts'[34] was the nearest equivalent in the Catholic Church to the fellowship body of an Oxford college. One of the reasons why

Manning felt doubtful about Newman's loyalty in tackling the needs of Roman Catholics, as he and Wiseman conceived them, was his suspicion that Newman had not, and could not, leave his old life behind. Newman's brand of Catholicism was 'the old Anglican, patristic, literary Oxford tone transplanted into the Church'.[35]

Perhaps this is what the Roman Catholic Church in England sorely needed. It is very questionable, however, whether it was what the newly-founded University for Ireland at Dublin required. The story of Newman's six-years Rectorship is a very sad one, fraught with misunderstandings at every turn. Was it to be an 'imperial university' for all Catholics who spoke the English tongue, or was it to be a much-needed university for the Catholic youth of Ireland, following the condemnation of mixed education in that predominantly Catholic country by the papal rescript of 1847? There is no doubt what the papal rescript intended; equally emphatic was the opinion of Archbishop Cullen that the needs of Ireland must come first. To Newman, however, the new University offered the alluring prospect of creating a second Oxford across the Irish Sea. 'Curious it will be', he mused in October 1851, 'if Oxford is imported into Ireland, not in its membership only, but in its principles, methods, ways and arguments.'[36]

This episode in Newman's career has been variously and controversially interpreted; almost as if any noble venture which ends in failure demands the identification of either a villain or a scapegoat. I find neither the one nor the other in my reading of the course of events. All three of the major figures in the story of the Irish University were men of integrity, and the actions and attitudes of each were entirely in conformity with their background and character. Newman was bound to be Oxford-inspired in his thinking, but this does not mean that he was dismissive of the genuine needs of the Irish. Archbishop Cullen had no experience of university education himself; he misunderstood Newman's determination to create a collegiate institution, with tutors exercising as important a role as the professorial staff; and by virtue of his position and character as a typical conservative ecclesiastic, fresh from the Rectorship of the Irish College in Rome, it was inevitable that he would not be prepared to give an inch in relaxing the overall control of the University by the hierarchy. John MacHale, Archbishop of Tuam, was an ardent Irish nationalist, who had every reason, from the experiences of the appalling consequences of the potato famine in his diocese, for distrusting the English. He regarded Newman's appointment as an insult to the Irish, and resented the condescension implicit in Newman's frequent references to his Oxford experiences and his appointment of Oxford converts to positions within the University. There was, then, an inevitability in the dashing of Newman's hopes.

Nevertheless what posterity has to cherish is the blue-print of what might have been in one of Newman's most moving and influential published writings, *The Idea of a University*. These nine discourses, especially the last five, were certainly Oxford-inspired, if more a picture of what Oxford had the potential to be than a description of the actuality. Those who have criticized Newman's vision as narrow or who have accused him of seeking to perpetuate a system which was already an anachronism in the 1850s cannot have studied closely the whole extensive range of his writings on what he hoped to achieve in Dublin. Quite apart from exhibiting in these a much more pragmatic understanding of the educational needs of the second half of the nineteenth century than is commonly allowed, he time and again emphasized one particular element, learnt from his Oxford and Oriel experience, the wisdom and sensitivity of which no one educated at Oxford, I fancy, would wish to challenge. 'An academic system', he wrote, 'without the personal influence of teachers upon pupils, is an arctic winter; it will create an ice-bound, petrified, cast-iron University, and nothing else.'[37]

As an expression of faith in the superiority of wisdom to knowledge, of the interrelation of the various disciplines of study, and as a declaration of the highest aims to which university education should aspire, *The Idea of a University* is a classic. 'It is the final utterance of Christian Humanism', G M Young once wrote; 'as if the spirit evoked by Erasmus had found its voice at last.'[38] And again, the same writer, in the course of his Foundation Oration at Birkbeck College, London, made the following unequivocal claim: 'If ever the Dark Ages return, and two books only come through, then, if those books are Aristotle's *Ethics* and Newman's *Idea of a University*, they will be enough to show a reviving world what civilisation meant.'[39] To Matthew Arnold it represented the quintessential Oxford tone of sentiment and its enduring rejection of Philistinism. These are Oxford tributes with, perhaps, more than a tinge of the Romantic about them. Nevertheless, I would venture to suggest that no one should be allowed to embark upon the framing of a National Curriculum until he had read Newman's discourses; if he discovered nothing else, he would at least encounter the only book on education in the English language which is a joy to read.

This is nearly my final remark on the subject of Newman and Oxford. One other episode remains, however, which should not be overlooked. In March 1856, Newman, musing over the failure of his Irish hopes, frankly admitted, 'I would far rather do good to English Catholics in Oxford than in Dublin',[40] because with the abolition of religious tests two years earlier, the admission of English Catholics to Oxford became a real possibility. At first Newman had his reservations, fearful of the effect of scepticism and infidelity upon the impressionable Catholic youth; also he did not want to be part of any process of introducing 'controversy into those quiet and sober circles . . . which are the strength of the Church of England'.[41] But when proposals for the foundation of a Catholic college in Oxford were mooted, despite the firm opposition of Manning and the majority of the hierarchy to the principle of mixed education (and perhaps, in part, because of it), Newman's opinions changed. The most likely scheme to be accepted by Propaganda was the establishment of a branch of the Birmingham Oratory as an Oxford mission; and to that end Newman, with the support of influential Catholic laymen, purchased land in Oxford, immediately envisaging the prospect of a return to the scene of his former triumphs. 'Such a man as Mark Pattison may conceivably be won over', he wrote in excitement in 1867. 'Although I am not young, I feel as full of life and thought as ever I did. It may prove to be the inauguration of a second Oxford Movement.'[42] Newman's bishop, Ullathorne, unhappily rather late in the day, then broke the news: Propaganda approved, on the condition, however, that Newman should not leave Birmingham. The Pope feared that Newman's presence at Oxford might prove a magnet to draw Catholics to that less than desirable place. Understandably, Newman was bitterly disappointed. He lost all interest in the establishment of a mission, and urged that the whole plan should be abandoned at once. The money (to purchase the land) had been given 'to *me* personally'.[43]

Newman was not to return to Oxford until 1877, when Trinity officially recognized the eminence of their once erring son. So the story does have a happy end in the twilight of his days. Oxford had been to Newman the scene of some of his bitterest disappointments both early in life, when he suffered his breakdown in the Schools, and in the course of his subsequent career – the dismissal from his tutorship, the condemnation by the Hebdomadal Board, the frustration of his plans to preside over the Oxford mission; but it had also been the arena of his greatest triumphs. It was there that he had enjoyed his time of plenty. Bearing in mind that his departure in 1845 was in the guise of a renegade, we must acknowledge that Oxford very quickly forgave him. It was almost as if they knew that he carried the love of the place for ever in his heart, whatever he may have said, from time to time, about his reluctance to return. Newman never forgot Oxford, and Oxford has never forgotten him. Even now, because his Oxford days have been memorialized so graphically and so eloquently by those who had the privilege of sitting at his feet, and because in Oxford one is surrounded by scenes and images that meant so much to him – the Adam de Brome chapel in St Mary's, the house at Littlemore, maybe even the upraised, accusatory finger of the Martyrs' Memorial so tactlessly close to Trinity, and maybe also the snapdragon that grew on the wall there, near to his room (does it grow there still?) – we may find ourselves from time to time tempted to picture in our minds' eye the figure whom history has enabled us to see so well and then to utter those six exquisitely poignant and evocative words of Matthew Arnold: 'I seem to hear him still . . .'

NOTES

1. M Arnold, 'Literature and Science', *Nineteenth Century* XII (August 1882), p. 218.
2. I Ker, *John Henry Newman* (Oxford 1988), p. 493.
3. Maisie Ward, *Young Mr Newman* (1948), p. 97.
4. G Rowell, *The Vision Glorious* (Oxford 1983), p. 49.
5. T M Parker, 'The rediscovery of the Fathers in the seventeenth-century Anglican tradition' in *The Rediscovery of Newman: an Oxford Symposium*, ed. J Coulson and A M Allchin (London, SPCK, 1967), pp. 31–49.
6. Ker, pp. 33–4.
7. *Letters and Diaries of J. H. Newman*, II, pp. 125–6.
8. *Apologia* (W Ward's edn 1913), p. 106.
9. G M Young, *Daylight and Champaign* (1957), p. 62.
10. *Apologia*, p. 174.

11. J T Coleridge, *Memoir of the Rev. John Keble* (1869), I, p. 73.
12. M Ward, pp. 180-1.
13. Ker, p. 711.
14. W Ward, *William George Ward and the Oxford Movement* (1889), p. 149.
15. W Ward, p. 219.
16. R W Church, *The Oxford Movement 1833-1845* (1891), p. 141.
17. D Newsome, *The Parting of Friends* (1966), p. 165.
18. C S Dessain, *John Henry Newman* (1966), p. 43.
19. M Arnold, *Discourses in America* (1912), p. 141.
20. Dessain, p. 44.
21. Ker, pp. 172, 163
22. W Ward, *Last Lectures* (1918), p. 52.
23. O Chadwick, *The Mind of the Oxford Movement* (1960), p. 54.
24. F L Cross, *John Henry Newman* (1933), p. 142.
25. *Difficulties of Anglicans* (1896 edn), II, p. 24.
26. Unpublished journals of Stopford Brooke, 24 January 1898.
27. M. Pattison, *Memoirs* (1885), pp. 235-6.
28. D J Delaura, 'Matthew Arnold and John Henry Newman' in *Texas Studies in Literature and Language*, Supp. to VI (1965), p. 587.
29. Ker, p. 344.
30. ibid., p. 512.
31. R Gray, *Cardinal Manning* (1985), p. 250.
32. J E C Bodley, *Cardinal Manning and other Essays* (1912), pp. 13-14.
33. Ker, p. 592.
34. ibid., pp. 429-30.
35. A C F Fawkes, *Quarterly Review* (April 1912), p. 466.
36. V A McClelland, *English Roman Catholics and Higher Education, 1830-1903* (Oxford 1973), p. 100.
37. F McGrath, *Newman's University. Idea and Reality* (1951), p. 337.
38. G M Young, *Last Essays* (1950), p. 100.
39. G M Young, *Today and Yesterday* (1948), p. 115.
40. McClelland, p. 119.
41. Ker, p. 493.
42. McClelland, p. 223.
43. ibid., p. 224.

· 3 ·

Newman's Significance for the Anglican Church

HENRY CHADWICK

The titles of this lecture and the next raise large issues both historically and in terms of Newman's current significance for the two communions: more than could reasonably be expected to be covered in a single lecture. As will be seen, Archbishop D'Arcy's solution is to illustrate that significance by focusing on a particular topical issue of the moment, while in his contribution Dr Chadwick takes us, in what follows, back to the historical context in which Newman's ideas as an Anglican were first developed. But what we have is no mere historical survey. Sometimes explicitly but again and again implicitly fellow Anglicans are challenged to reflect upon their understanding of the Church (particularly its sacramental character) and upon the related issue of the doctrine of justification and Newman's ecumenical understanding of it.

In the early 1830s a young Fellow of Oriel, possessed of rare literary powers but (as Routh the old President of Magdalen remarked) evidently modest ambitions for success in his career, became convinced that the liberalism of the eighteenth century Enlightenment and the Evangelical Revival had combined to cause much of the Church of England to forget its catholic inheritance in Hooker, Andrewes, Laud, Cosin, and Thorndike. With a heterogeneous group of allies among the Oriel dons, he set out to recall this Church to the rock whence it was hewn. He met with astonishing and lasting success, but also with fierce opposition and even panic. Hooker had accepted that the Roman Catholic Church was a true Church, though not flawless (the sixteenth-century term for that was 'corrupt'). With a mounting crescendo Newman's question came to be whether this entailed the conclusion that the Anglican Church either must be, or could be empirically shown to be, a Catholic sham. Finally he gave his allegiance to Rome for the second half of his life. Apart from Manning, compiler of a catena from the Church Fathers in Tract 78, he was the only Tract writer to shift his allegiance.

'All I can say is', said Keble, 'that if the Roman Church is the one true Church, I do not know it.' After Keble's death Newman liked to quote his words as illustrating the principle of invincible ignorance, and proving that the saintly Keble would get to heaven.[1]

Newman's exodus did not end, though it damaged, the Tractarian revival. The changes that he more than any other man brought about in Anglicanism were far greater than those which he likewise tried to bring about in the Roman Catholic Church, within which he came to reckon his life a miserable failure – while never doubting that he was where he ought to be.[2] Some things he said before 1845 sounded Romish to Anglicans. After 1845 he incurred jealousy and distrust by sounding so Anglican and English.[3] His influence within the Roman Catholic Church was largely posthumous; during his lifetime he was suspected and marginalized. Within the Anglican Communion his influence was profound, and in virtually all his writings including those after 1845 (except for *Loss and Gain*, the autobiographical novel of 1848 where there is a touch of 'convertitis'), Anglican readers feel at home.

The subject given to me is Newman's significance for Anglicans, and to understand that it is necessary to begin with what was characteristic of faith and piety in the England of Newman's youth, the age of the industrial revolution and of Benthamite utilitarianism in which 'tradition' was a leaden word.

The fierce Protestantism of the Revolution of 1689 had associated Catholicism with much more than religion. It meant the power of Louis XIV, revocation of the Edict of Nantes, arbitrary autocracy, wretched conditions for the poor. The Revolution weakened the special relationship of Church and Crown (further damaged in 1714 with the accession of a German to whom the Prayer Book was incomprehensible). Above all, it was bad news not only for Roman Catholics but also for the high Anglicans prominent at the Restoration. Respect for ancient liturgies and a sacramental Church became a mark of Non-jurors, ejected from the Church by their conscientious inability to swear allegiance to William of Orange. Non-jurors became prominent in the rebuttal of the ferociously anticlerical Deists. Nevertheless, in the eighteenth century Church of England, two antithetical groups dominated the age: (1) the Latitudinarians or Liberals, men like Hoadly Bishop of Bangor for whom the Church was in effect the religious department of the government, an instrument for social control and amelioration, putting a gentleman into each parish, but not the transmitter of a divine word of redemption; (2) the pietists or Evangelicals, who flourished especially in soil fertilized by Calvinism and then, with John Wesley, acquired the power to flourish almost equally well in a more liberal Arminian milieu, more congenial perhaps to an instinctive high Anglican like Wesley.

Both the Latitudinarians and the Evangelicals were in reaction against the religious conflicts and wars of the seventeenth century, and shared a dislike of theological intricacies: the liberals regarded dogmatic or revealed theology as narrow, the Evangelicals regarded it as spiritually desiccating. Justification by faith had been Luther's grand theme; but the amazing complexity of this matter brought fierce controversies within the Lutheran camp in Germany, culminating in that highly divisive declaration, the *Formula of Concord*. The eighteenth-century Evangelicals hated the intricate disputes, and wanted to believe that justification was 'the simple gospel'; that justifying faith is a purely inward feeling of trust; that the elect can know themselves to be elect by the feeling of assurance imparted to them by their trust in Christ. Because of the sympathy some of them felt for John Calvin, they also inherited a deep reserve towards the visible structures of the Church, towards any concept of mediation other than through the historic incarnation and through the Bible; in short there was no special mediation through the sacraments, which were moral aids to piety but not the only ordinary means to their respective graces.

Under the influence of an Evangelical schoolmaster at his school in Ealing, Newman experienced an adolescent conversion, and for a time was a moderate Calvinist (not of course of the extreme or Toplady school). The anniversary of this conversion was kept, even after his becoming a Roman Catholic.

Newman's engagement with popular Evangelicalism is at its

most profound in his book on justification, published in 1838, originating as lectures in Adam de Brome's chapel at St Mary the Virgin. It is by general consent acknowledged to be his most remarkable theological book, though deliberately addressed to the general reader in largely untechnical language. He read widely and deeply in the controversial works of the sixteenth and seventeenth centuries and, though ignorant of German and even of the history of the Reformation in Germany,[4] found his way to writings by Luther and Melanchthon. He ended with the conviction that those who hold justification to be on the ground of the imputing of Christ's righteousness and those who hold that we are justified by the imparting of that righteousness are not as incompatible as they like to think. Believers are justified not by a Protestant 'faith alone', nor by the degree of inward renewal under grace, but by the indwelling Christ in the soul (the doctrine encapsulated in one verse of 'Praise to the holiest in the height', beginning 'And that a higher gift than grace, should flesh and blood refine . . .'). The formal cause of justification is God's grace and mercy, not a human act of faith. Evangelicals of the time commonly supposed that, by Reformation principles, justification 'by faith alone' necessarily excludes all means of grace through the God-given sacraments or divinely commissioned ministers (a proposition expressly denied in the Lutheran *Apology for the Augsburg Confession*, 1531). They suffered embarrassment in being unable to give a clear content to the term faith, and in being able only to say what it is not, such as intellectual assent or any kind of moral quality. But if faith is trust, it is paradoxical to assert that no element of love enters into it. Moreover, it is a mistake to set asunder forgiveness and inner renewal: they are simultaneous, not successive. Newman saw (was perhaps the first theologian to see) that Protestant language about the imputed merits of Christ being the believer's only hope is, in another idiom, saying what Catholics affirm in the doctrine of the sacrifice of the Mass: 'The Father looking on us sees not us but Christ in us.'[5]

The warm Evangelicalism of Newman's adolescence and undergraduate years left a permanent mark, but soon was succeeded by a more Liberal phase. His election to be a Fellow of Oriel brought him into the most brilliant intellectual circle in the Oxford of 1822. Tongue-tied and shy, he was fascinated by Richard Whately the logician, an uncouth person who upset his colleagues by spitting into the common room fire, but who stretched Newman's mind by sharp rationalism and antipathy to superstition, whether Catholic or Protestant.

To the end of his days, long after he had found inadequate the obsessive -isms of Evangelical Calvinism and its fascination with the interpretation of the Apocalypse, Newman would speak and write with respect and admiration for individual Evangelicals as men and women of great devotion, seriousness, and holiness. Through them God had 'touched his heart'. What they had not done was to touch his mind. Whately, he said in the *Apologia*,[6] taught him to think.

Whately wanted the Church of England to be more independent of Parliament and Crown. In the anonymously published *Letters on the Church* of 1826 (the authorship of which he never actually admitted but which Newman unhesitatingly ascribed to him),[7] Whately indicted Parliament as altogether incompetent to act as a house of laity for the Church. 'If anyone doubts the possibility of finding in eminent statesmen the grossest ignorance of the doctrines and institutions of the Church of England, let him read the speeches in parliament on the Catholic question.'[8] Protestant as he was, and the more so after he became Archbishop of Dublin in 1831, Whately saw what simplistic nonsense it was to say that where Protestants teach justification by faith, Rome teaches justification by works; or that it is any objection to transubstantiation that the senses perceive no change.[9] Whately urged that the untenability of Roman Catholicism was shown rather by its too soft yielding to popular superstitions and by its too hard claims to infallibility. But such grounds were not easily maintained by a conservative Protestant Evangelical, whose beliefs about the Bible looked to a liberal strikingly marked by infallibilism and near-superstition.

For the young Newman, Whately's conversation was heady stuff. He became fascinated by Whately's insistence that much controversy is rooted in logical and verbal confusions. In a University Sermon of 6 January 1839 Newman declared: 'Half the controversies in the world are verbal ones; and could they be brought to a plain issue, they would be brought to a prompt termination . . . We need not dispute, we need not prove, – we need but define . . . When men understand each other's meaning, they see, for the most part, that controversy is either superfluous or hopeless.'[10] In these words we seem to hear Whately and Newman agreeing together, even after they had drifted apart.

But Whately was not the only influential figure in the Oriel common room. John Keble the poet, son of an old-style high churchman, supremely modest and self-effacing, was tenacious in adherence to the Anglican tradition of Hooker, Laud, Bramhall, and Jeremy Taylor (though a bit uncertain about Taylor), unsympathetic to Bentham, Mill, and progressivist voices.[11] When in 1864 Pope Pius IX appalled liberal society by producing the *Syllabus of Errors*, Newman remarked that the Syllabus was what John Keble had always thought.[12] A third don at Oriel brought Keble and Newman to understand one another, Hurrell Froude: provocative, blaming the state control of the Church brought in by the Reformation for the sad condition of things, but equally hostile both to the Reformers and to the anti-Reformation Council of Trent. His dislike of the English Reformers as characters was qualified only by his admiration for the matchless beauty of the Prayer Book.[13] Froude's conversation had a catalytic effect on Newman. Both men loved Walter Scott's novels with their rose-coloured picture of medieval times.[14]

Froude contended that Erastian subservience to government lay at the heart of the Church of England's ineffectiveness, and thought it made the Church of England preach to the English not the apostolic faith but what the English felt they wanted to believe. Their criterion of truth was what Englishmen found congenial. Froude's suspicion of Erastianism led him to a prolonged study of Becket's resistance to Henry II (*Remains* IV). He studied ancient liturgies, confident that the indeed ancient Latin mass is a text first composed by St Peter himself (an opinion echoed by Newman later).[15] Froude longed for Canterbury and Rome to recover the spirit of the ancient Fathers, abandoned by Rome at Trent and by the Reformers when they treated the sacraments to rationalistic disparagement. Yet in the classical records of Anglican tradition Froude knew there was a powerful ingredient of faith and practice that can only be called Catholic. Cannot Anglicans once again speak, as did Hooker and Bishop Bull, of a power to make the body and blood of Christ being vested in the apostles' successors? Or with Hammond of the Church as an infallible transmitter and guardian of the faith? Or with William Law of the sacramentality of ordination? Froude admired Catholic ideals, not Roman actuality. But a note in his journal asks how we can know that Rome's changes from ancient practice are not a valid 'development of the apostolic ethos'.[16] He insisted on giving full value to the preface to the Thirty-Nine Articles enjoining that they are to be taken in their literal and grammatical sense, and saw that this did not mean that Cranmer's wobbly personal beliefs provided a rule for their interpretation. In short, the Articles of the Church of England are patient if not ambitious of a Catholic interpretation, a phrase from Froude which was like an arrow piercing Newman's mind.[17]

Hurrell Froude invited Newman to come on his Mediterranean trip during December 1832 and the early months of 1833. Never in good health, he died aged 33 on 28 February 1836, leaving a candid and intimate journal about his opinions and ascetic mortifications to quell temptation. Newman admired and loved Froude, but feared a plan to publish his journal and papers. Other Tractarian friends overrode his misgivings: publication would show a true saint, and his sharp sayings would make people think hard. Newman's misgivings were justified. The publication was disastrous for the Tractarian cause. Evangelicals, meeting at Islington in January 1837, were already denouncing Pusey as a heretic.[18] Now their worst suspicions were confirmed.

Froude's influence amplified an ascetic, almost monastic inclination latent in Newman's soul. A true Christian profession must be world-renouncing. Only God and the soul matter, not friends or relatives.[19] Already at the Evangelical adolescent stage of development Newman knew himself called to remain unmarried. As Vicar of St Mary the Virgin his sermons summon his hearers to profound penitence. Public demand led him to print his parish sermons. Of the first volume Samuel Wilberforce wrote to complain that it induced fear and depression. Newman replied that in the present parlous state of the Church of England, sermons and services ought to be 'a continual Ash Wednesday'.[20] There is more pity than fear, but Newman was no doubt inclined to exaggerate how parlous things were. But his pastoral experience as Vicar of St Mary the Virgin convinced him that the Evangelicals' emotional creed could produce disaster. He knew of prayer meetings that had ended in fornication.[21]

Justification by faith alone was being interpreted to mean by feeling alone. Did Luther find humanity in bondage to good works and liberate them only to bring them into bondage to their feelings? At least the Evangelicals had implanted in his mind a conviction of the absoluteness of the Christian revelation, and therefore a reaction against the prevalent relativism which saw all religious positions as equally true to their adherents, equally untrue to others, so that the only real criterion must be the sincerity with which the positions were held.

Keble's influence directed Newman to the rich mine of intelligence and spirituality in Hooker and the seventeenth-century Caroline divines. His Assize Sermon[22] taught him that the Church does not need the State to be itself, and should make its own decisions, for example about the appointment of bishops.

The student of St Augustine soon discovers that the man's heart is most transparently disclosed not in his great formal treatises, not in his polemical tracts against heretics and schismatics, against Donatists, Manichees, and Pelagians, but rather in the sermons he preached to his regular congregation of dockworkers and agricultural labourers, the sermons on the Psalms and on St John. So too with Newman. The heart of the Anglican Newman is not found in the writer of brilliant hard-hitting controversy, the author of the *Prophetical Office of the Church* with its vigorous attacks on both Rome and Protestantism. By 'Protestant', Newman meant something essentially negative, vague about positive beliefs, only incisive about what we doubt, deny, ridicule or resist.[23]

Newman never writes more brilliantly than when summarizing a position with which he disagrees. *The Prophetical Office* is a potent, even strident statement of the Via Media, the middle path between that excess of authority in Rome and the lack of it in the Reformation bodies. One does not have to read between the lines to see that Newman thinks authentic Anglicanism closer to Roman Catholicism than to popular Protestantism.[24] Yet with Rome there remains a divide: 'If we advance to Rome as a sister or mother Church, we shall find too late that we are in the arms of a pitiless and unnatural relative'.[25] The denial of the cup to the laity,[26] popular Marian devotions that encroach on the honour of Mary's Son,[27] an excess of dogmatic anathemas, seem to the Newman of the Via Media a barrier to the acceptance of Rome. But it is, he thinks, a foolish error to suppose that authority can lie in Scripture alone apart from the interpretation given by tradition in the witness of the community. And if as some Protestants long to hold, the sense of Scripture is clear, how is it that Protestantism has begotten so many sects with incompatible opinions?

The Prophetical Office of the Church was written at a time when some critics were beginning to express alarm that the Tractarian stress on the visible Church and sacraments would in the end lead them to Rome. Puritans had said that about seventeenth-century Caroline divinity in Laud and Bramhall and Taylor, and received from Bramhall the tart reply that, among Puritans, conversions to Rome much exceeded those among Prayer Book using Anglicans. The Tractarians were felt as a threat because for a century neither Liberal nor Evangelical had said anything about the universal Church. To proclaim that article of the Creed was sure to precipitate a row.

The Roman Catholic community in England had been steadily increasing. They grew from about 80,000 in the 1760s to three-quarters of a million by 1851.[28] Irish immigrants strengthened the working class churchgoers, largely absent from the Church of England. The Tractarians, then, were not hoping to strengthen the Roman Catholic Church. The Romeward movement had a quite independent existence. Newman after 1845, Manning after 1852, and other converts injected a high culture and intelligence into a community which needed more of these assets. Though figures like Lord Acton should warn against exaggeration, it is broadly true that the converts transformed the situation, and caused offence to old Catholic families by failing to conceal their pleasure in that fact. Newman's distinctive and personal contribution after 1845, perhaps, was to demonstrate that it was possible to be in communion with Rome and to be a hundred per cent English.

The Tractarians were misread by Evangelicals and Liberals when they were credited with a conspiratorial intention to get Canterbury to submit to Rome. They actually feared the Roman Catholic revival and were alarmed by the defencelessness of Anglicanism if its theology was either Liberal or Calvinist Evangelical. Their ideal was Catholicism without universal papal jurisdiction. But they were uncomfortable with some popular devotions admitted by Rome; and most of those in the Tractarian tradition, including Pusey and Keble, accepted the legitimacy of a married priesthood. A married priesthood was not, of course, any barrier to the acknowledgement of the validity of orders; witness Roman recognition of Orthodox orders. But conversion to Rome was a high barrier to a priest with a wife, unless he wished to find an escape from pastoral responsibility.

The group which conceived the plan of Tracts for the Times was miscellaneous with very diverse backgrounds, not at all tightly knit. There were significant differences among them. Newman was acutely conscious of his differences from Pusey, less so of those from Keble. They did not all share the same estimate of the Reformation, though it is safe to say that none of them sacralized the sixteenth century as the breaking out of light after fifteen centuries of Stygian darkness, surely the most improbable of all interpretations of church history.

The early Tracts achieved a success that astonished the group. They sold widely among parish clergy. But in Oxford itself, the grand draw lay not in the Tracts or editions of Anglican classics, but in the sermons of the Vicar of St Mary the Virgin, delivered on Sunday afternoons at 4.00 or 5.00. These discourses drew an ever increasing crowd from the more thoughtful and bookish stratum of the undergraduates.[29] (A letter to James Stephen, written in February 1835, mentions with surprise that his sermons were found attractive by women, 'who do not reason and only feel').[30] Contemporaries had become bored by the predictability of repetitive Evangelical preachers with their favoured themes of original sin, justification by faith, the atonement, the feeling of being assured of pardon and final perseverance. The Liberals like Hampden, the Regius Professor, had no real belief in the presence of Christ to his people in the sacramental life of the Church, no sense of mystery in divine revelation, and were much inclined to suggest or imply that Unitarians were just as good Christians as those who adhered to the incarnation and the Trinity, and indeed that all sects felt the same truth which they were expressing in different ways.

Newman's sermons are very unlike an Evangelical seeking to melt his hearers and move them to conversion. But they are strikingly biblical. More than one contemporary witness tells of the riveting way in which he used to read the lessons from Scripture. As a preacher he had no tricks of rhetoric. He kept his eyes buried in his carefully composed script. Yet his congregation was utterly held, and it was not comfortable stuff to hear. Apart from some satirical passages[31] there were no witticisms, few sharp epigrams or particularly striking utterances, but always a profound intensity on two central themes: that the good moral life is of the substance of

worship, and that the Church and sacraments are not optiona
extras or marginal ceremonies that serious Christians can use or no
use according to their fancy, but essential to the gospel: 'Forms are
the food of faith'.[32]

Every sermon has a potent scriptural content. But Newman was
clear that Scripture is not self-explanatory. It needs an authorized
interpreter. If an inquirer asks the Archbishop of Canterbury what
the Church of England believes on this or that major issue, and i
the answer he receives is to the effect that for the Church of England
the sole authority is the Bible which each believer is free to interpret
as he feels led or inclined, the conclusion is almost irresistible that
this Church does not know what it believes.[33]

Newman's hearers at the time felt that his sermons had little
High Church theology, but were directed to moral issues. The
reader of the printed text can quickly discern that they were learning
much about the Church, about apostolic succession, about baptism
and Holy Communion as mediating the very presence of the Lord
and his sacrifice,[34] but these themes are integrated into the grand
theme of the necessity of reality and the quest for authentic holiness.
The sacramental ecclesiology is there because of the means of grace
and sanctification. The Lord gave sacraments because we need
them, and we need them because they bring to us the grace and help
necessary for the path to a sober, righteous, and holy life.

A letter of 27 January 1846 to Henry Wilberforce recalls that
Newman used to give private absolution according to the form in
the Visitation of the Sick in the Prayer Book, and that at the early
Eucharist at St Mary's he 'had an absolute and overpowering sense
of the Real Presence'. Newman did not first learn these things after
becoming convinced that Rome has the Truth. They came to him
out of the native Anglican tradition.

The St Mary's sermons are dominated by the quest for reality in
religion. Strip away worldly compromises. Obey conscience, the
very voice of God. In rational judgements second thoughts are often
best, but not in matters of conscience where first thoughts are
right.[35] There is no more exquisite pain in human life than that of a
bad conscience, and murderers have preferred to die at the
executioner's hand than to live with the memory of what they did.
How many live lives haunted by the ghosts of the past, by sins
brushed aside unconfessed and still unabsolved.[36] Newman's
pastoral labours at St Mary's convinced him that there was danger

or even catastrophe in telling people that a personal sense of assurance is the criterion of being one of God's elect,[37] and that there is no mortal sin other than lack of faith.[38]

To put such stress on feeling to the neglect of the ethical encourages superficiality. England, the richest country in the world,[39] is dominated by the appetite for wealth and power,[40] 'For the sake of gain, do we not put aside all considerations of principle as . . . absurd? . . . Is there any speculation in commerce which religion is allowed to interfere with? . . . Do we care what side of a quarrel, civil, political, or international, we take, so that we gain by it? . . . Do we not support religion for the sake of peace and good order . . . [and] only in so far as it procures them?'[41] People think the function of religion is simply to turn out good citizens and no more.[42] So the profession of the ordained ministry is regarded as comfortable.[43] In one sermon of March 1840 Newman allowed himself an express observation that, without questioning the legitimacy and propriety of marriage for the clergy, nevertheless there is a higher dedication possible to the celibate.[44] The domestic virtue of the parsonage family is admirable; but Newman regrets the rarity of the heroic in the Anglican ideal.[45]

To Latitudinarians and to many Evangelicals, sacraments were either merely symbolic reminders akin to visual aids or, if supposed to be more than that, perilously akin to superstition. In the 1820s it was still common for Holy Communion to be celebrated in a Church of England parish church only at Easter, Pentecost, and Christmas, the three being the minimum number specified by rubric in the Prayer Book for communicants.[46] Daily services were unusual. At St Mary's Newman established an early weekly celebration, Communion on saints' days, and daily mattins and evensong (here following the high Anglican tradition represented by Keble).[47] Newman was never interested in ceremonial or vestments, but by 1837 some of the Tractarian followers were beginning to look that way: in 1837 two Fellows at Magdalen took to wearing a stole.[48] Newman thought it a hindrance to Catholic recovery when followers 'become peculiar in externals' and practise 'ostentatious fasts'.[49] When people saw popery in bowing to the altar, Newman could reply that at Christ Church the Dean and Canons had long done so by immemorial tradition.[50]

The controversies that came to rage round Newman's head in 1841–2 left him sore. Any lie about him found ready credence. Yet why was he being censured for reasserting the beliefs of Laud or Bramhall, acknowledged pillars of Anglican ecclesiology and certainly no papists? The storm broke with Tract 90 in February 1841: the Thirty-Nine Articles, interpreted with hairsplitting exactitude in their literal and grammatical sense, were subordinate to and no rejection of Catholic tradition; only they are not wrong to question universal papal jurisdiction and to affirm the Real Presence without conceding transubstantiation. Tract 90 was more Anglican than it was represented to be; not much was said there which had not been quietly and less ingeniously said by Pusey in an open *Letter to the Bishop of Oxford* published two years earlier. Pusey disliked the manner of Tract 90. Newman's delight in exact logic made the argument sound clever, enjoyably so if you wanted to agree, evasively sophisticated if you did not. For example, people thought sophistry the observation that Article 22, which criticizes the invocation of saints, does not deny their intercession for us in that one communion and fellowship in which God has knit together his elect. They were nettled if told that the Benedicite ('O ye spirits and souls of the righteous') has an invocation. That there might be dangers Newman could readily concede.

Tract 90 was written to put a brake on over-enthusiastic followers urging that the claim of Rome was irresistible. Prominent among these was William George Ward, Mathematics Tutor at Balliol and logician; acute in conversation, confused and soggy as a writer, he proposed to cure the Church of England of its ills by radical Romanization, including both obligatory auricular confession and the Marian devotions of St Alfonso Liguori. Ward had in youth attended Roman Catholic services, and the fever was not implanted in him by Newman. But he claimed to be taking Newman's principles to their ultimate conclusion, asserting the right to interpret the Articles in a 'non-natural' sense, a view which Newman disowned.[51] Newman could reasonably point out that he remained opposed to removing the old Oxford requirement of assent to the Articles, and that if he was asking for latitude of interpretation here and there, his difficulties with the Articles were trivial compared with Evangelical embarrassment with the Prayer Book order for infant baptism or the absolution in the Visitation of the Sick or with the very uncalvinist Article 16. He had spoken of 'the stammering lips of ambiguous formularies'. Did not all admit that Article 17 on predestination was acceptable to both Calvinist and Arminian?

Newman was asking for much less liberty than the Liberals. He felt sad to see how in the Church of England there is toleration for any beliefs except affirmations of Catholic truth[52] (a view which received astringent expression in *Loss and Gain*).

During 1841, with the major exception of the highly intelligent Bishop Thirlwall at St David's,[53] bishops fulminated against Tract 90. Even his own Bishop of Oxford, Richard Bagot, who endured hostility for giving support to the Tractarians, became intimidated into uttering words of mild regret. The immunological system of the Church of England was rejecting Newman as an alien intruder; Newman deduced that its self-understanding was to abjure a Catholic understanding of the Church and sacraments, which a Protestant Establishment must spontaneously vomit forth. Invite this Church to enjoy its Catholic inheritance, and instinctively it will scuttle for cover. The hammering charges of bishops (he called it a 'war dance') convinced the always touchy Newman that the Church of England did not now wish to be reminded of its Catholic heritage in Thorndike, Taylor or Sanderson. The anger and hurt felt by Newman, especially at insinuations that he lacked honesty and integrity, were so great that it took time for him to feel sure of his motives in wishing to become a Roman Catholic: he must not be converted merely because there are unreasonable people in the Anglican communion.[54] There was of course a positive pull to Rome in Newman's quest for mystery, awe, reverence, the reality of a religion where God comes to humanity through his own appointed sacramental signs. As he lost confidence, he came to think Anglican worship dreary.

At the same time Newman was drawn to Rome by his patristic studies, by idiosyncratic arguments from his readings in the ancient Fathers. Was the autocephaly of the Church of England analogous to the schismatic Donatists in fourth-century North Africa, or to the Egyptian Monophysites of the sixth?[55] In his retreat at Littlemore he translated Athanasius, and his notes to that translation show him torn between his admiration for Bishop Bull and his anxiety that emperor-toadying Arians like Eusebius of Caesarea were Erastian Anglicans before the latter. To Pusey and Keble such arguments seemed bizarre. Indeed, Newman himself knew that the Catholic denial of validity to Anglican sacraments was anticipated by the Donatist denial of validity to all Catholic sacraments; Bramhall had taught him that.

In 1841 Wiseman at Oscott nursed hopes that Tract 90 might facilitate a lowering of barriers to communion between Canterbury and Rome. Newman visited Wiseman high with optimism, but was cast down by the answer that it was not enough to show that the council of Trent and the Thirty-Nine Articles were compatible; the Church of England would need formally to accept the decrees of Trent as the principle for interpreting the Articles. Thereafter his hope that help might come from the Roman side faded. Nevertheless, Newman the Anglican Tractarian was not wrong to point out that the Anglican tradition, especially in the Ordinal and the Prayer Book when properly used as intended, was unintelligible apart from essentially Catholic elements. He was not wrong in holding that the Thirty-Nine Articles (so hostile to Baptists) are less Protestant than many in 1830 and later wished to believe, or in observing that the term 'Protestant' never occurs in Prayer Book or Articles. In both halves of his life Newman brought Anglican and Roman Catholic closer together, as he himself was to write in a letter of 15 October 1874.[56]

His treatment of the Thirty-Nine Articles in Tract 90 is logically much akin to his *Letter to the Duke of Norfolk* (1875) in which he proposed a 'legitimate minimizing' of the first Vatican Council on papal primacy, presented as an attack on Gladstone but, as everyone in the know realized, in fact attacking Manning. Anglicans believe that the Church has reliably transmitted the word and sacraments, since 'The Church has authority in matters of faith' (Art.20). Then is it extravagant to hold that St Peter's successor has a privileged position in articulating the faith of the universal Church and in providing an organ of decision? Vatican I did not affirm popes to be inspired, only to be negatively protected on grave issues at critical times from leading the Church astray; and it is proper to ascribe such authority to the head of the episcopal college.

Although initially doubting the authority of a council so far from unanimity, and explicitly regretting that it made much harder the task of converting people to Catholicism, Newman was far more positive about Vatican I than Acton, for whom the decree affirming that the pope had supreme authority apart from the bishops was a problem which might be explained hereafter but was not now clear enough for internal assent.[57] But Newman explicitly anticipated the judgement of the majority at Vatican II that Vatican I was onesided and incomplete, needing a parallel statement about the episcopate.

His *Letter to the Duke of Norfolk* caused almost as much *frisson* in Rome as Tract 90 had once done in Oxford.[58]

But my subject is not Newman and Rome but Newman and Canterbury. He put two weighty questions to the Anglican Communion which have not lost force. Although in the Church of England some have always held that an alteration in, say, the creed or sacraments or ministry would alter its being (not only what it has but what it is), others have held with Edmund Burke[59] that, like any other body corporate, the Church may change her laws without altering her identity, and this coheres with the right of reformation asserted in the sixteenth century without requiring the consent of others. So Newman restates Hurrell Froude's question: Does the ambition of the Church of England to be national lead it to feel so relatively indifferent to the claims of the universal as to have the unconscious consequence that Anglicans make their Church correspond to what the English wish to believe about themselves; that is, a wet and tolerant body, adhering to Christian tradition but remaining free in private judgement, not greatly interested in the notion of a visible Church that faithfully teaches a given revelation defined by Bible and sacred tradition? Anglicanism is periodically threatened by a Do-it-yourself spirit of consumer choice. And the ideal of a national Church can glide into making the Church a social instrument of government for secular ends. (Not that there are no analogies to that in Catholic tradition.)

Secondly, Newman's opaque musings about ancient Donatists and Monophysites veil a more substantial question. The Anglican Communion claims to be a branch of the one Catholica, but does not always know how to behave as such, does not easily recognize that the rights thus asserted imply duties. The Thirty-Nine Articles do not assert the pope to be Antichrist; in denying his universal jurisdiction they concede that he is at least lawful bishop of Rome. Yet all over the world Anglicanism is found to be in rivalry to the Catholica, offering, in Newman's cutting phrase, 'a mimicry of Catholicism'. Can it be the divine intention that branches of the Catholica be out of communion with each other?

The force of these two questions may be considerably mitigated if one notices how little thought Newman's concept of the Church gives to the ancient orthodox Churches of the east, who remain largely beyond his horizon and knowledge. They represent a living Catholic body, yet without papal jurisdiction. It caused them pain

67

when Vatican II not only reasserted but even enhanced the supremacy of the pope over the episcopate generally.

Underlying this last question lies the central and most intricate problem of the contemporary ecumenical movement (so much misunderstood by those who think ecumenism a polite name for treachery), namely the question of the nature and being of the Church founded upon the apostles and prophets. 550 years ago at Florence a large-hearted pope was able briefly to restore communion between the Greek East and the Latin West on the basis that, within one Catholic Church recognizing Roman primacy, differing traditions can be legitimate. If Newman was not a typical Tractarian (as indeed he was not), that is because he did not think about these issues in the same way as Keble and Pusey; and his concept of the Church after 1845 could make room for neither Canterbury nor eastern patriarchs. But if, as Manning thought, he was an untypical, rather too Anglican type of Roman Catholic, that is essentially because he did not think it a necessary or authentic mark of Catholicism to be authoritarian, centralized, intolerant, and legalistically juridical. (I take that to be the crucial sense in which Newman anticipated the convictions of the majority of bishops at the time of the Second Vatican Council.) With this remark I begin to encroach on Archbishop Eric D'Arcy's territory in the next essay.

NOTES

The following abbreviations are used:
LD *Letters and Diaries of John Henry Newman*, ed. C S Dessain et al. (Oxford University Press, 1961–84).
PPS *Parochial and Plain Sermons* (1868 edition): 8 vols.
VM Via Media (1896 edition): 2 vols.

1. LD XXVI, pp. 299, 364.
2. J H Newman, *Autobiographical Writings*, ed. Henry Tristram (1956), pp. 254–5: 'How forlorn and dreary has been my course since I have been a Catholic! Here has been the contrast — as a Protestant, I felt my religion dreary, not my life — but as a Catholic, my life dreary, not my religion . . . I doubt whether I can point to any joyful event of this world besides my scholarship at Trinity and my fellowship at Oriel — but since I have been a Catholic, I seem to myself to have had nothing but failure, personally' (1863).

Only the last decade, in a glow as Honorary Fellow of Trinity and then astonishingly a Cardinal, during which years he did nothing but say his prayers, was a time of recognition in the Church of his adoption. The sermons and letters before 1841 do not suggest that, prior to his loss of confidence in the Church of England, Newman found Prayer Book services dreary.

3. James Bryce, by upbringing an Ulster Presbyterian, in February 1875 when he was Regius Professor of Civil Law at Oxford, called on Newman at the Birmingham Oratory, and found him 'not a priest in his manner – still an Englishman more than a R. Catholic' (LD XXVII, p. 238n). In the *Letter to the Duke of Norfolk* (1875) Newman wrote of there being 'no inconsistency in being a good Catholic and a good Englishman' (*Diff. Angl.* II, p. 177). A letter of 1866 from Manning to Monsignor Talbot in Rome complained of Newman's Catholic writings: 'It is the old Anglican, patristic, literary, Oxford tone transplanted into the Church' (Purcell's *Life of Manning*, 1896, II, p. 323). A letter of 1847 records how old Catholic families regarded the Oxford converts with 'cold curiosity' (LD XII, p. 19).

After 9 October 1845 English Protestants quickly brought the accusation that for many years past Newman had been a secret Romanist plotting against the Church of his baptism, and soon Henry Wilberforce was begging Newman to send a disavowal (LD XII, pp. 19–20). That in the 1830s Newman held Catholic doctrine concerning eucharistic presence and sacrifice, priesthood, apostolic succession, and (in the main) justification is beyond doubt. But he moved only slowly and with reluctance to the view that the Roman Catholic Church is, simply, the one authentic communion, all others being in schism or heresy or both. Episcopal denunciations of Tract 90 were causative in convincing him that only Rome taught and guarded Catholic truth. 'If all the world agrees in telling a man he has no business in our Church, he will at length begin to think he has none' (6 March 1842, *Keble Corresp.*, p. 187). A long time at Littlemore was required to convince him that his motive for becoming a Roman Catholic was not mixed with anger at the English Church's dreadful treatment of him (passionately expressed in his sermon on the parting of friends). He could not justify himself in moving from one branch of the Catholic Church to another branch that might seem preferable. He had to feel convinced that 'Catholicism is a different religion' (LD XII, p. 224), and that Anglicans cannot be part of the Church if they do not condemn Adoptionists and Agnoetae, or if they fail to teach purgatorial fire and the need for clerical celibacy (ibid., p. 235).

4. Tract 38 (VM II, p. 20) and a letter of July 1834 (LD IV, p. 314) show Newman to have supposed that in 1530 the Diet of Augsburg approved the Lutheran Confession. On the recalling of the anniversary of his evangelical conversion, after his conversion to Rome, see LD XI, p. 252 of 24 September 1846.

5. *Lectures on (the doctrine of) Justification*, 3rd edn, p. 161. Newman's *Lectures on Justification* (1838) went through five editions in his lifetime (1840, 1874, 1885, 1890). I have discussed the argument of

the book in the volume *Newman after a Hundred Years*, edited by I T Ker and A G Hill (Oxford 1990). A masterly study of Evangelicals is Boyd Hilton's *The Age of Atonement* (Oxford 1988).

6. Chap. 1; cf. LD XV, pp. 175–9. Spitting: LD XXII, pp. 217–18. His distaste for liberalism led him strangely to deny having even read Whately's *Logic* (LD XXVI, p. 164) to which he had actually contributed.

7. LD IV, p. 189. Newman (LD IV, p. 165) agreed with Whately on the unsuitability of Parliament for governing church matters.

8. R Whately, *Letters on the Church* (1826), p. 174.

9. See Whately's *Romanism* (1878 edn), pp. 48–49; *Thoughts on Christian moral Instruction*, Charge, 1854, p. 13.

10. *Univ. Sermons* x, p. 200.

11. See W J A M Beek, *John Keble's literary and religious Contribution to the Oxford Movement* (Nijmegen 1959), and thereon Owen Chadwick's review in *JTS* ns 11 (1960), p. 429.

12. LD XXI, p. 378.

13. *Remains* I, p. 35, a note of 1 November 1826.

14. Froude, *Rem.* I, p. 379; a letter from Newman in Anne Mozley's edition, II, p. 403. Allusions to Scott's Novels are not infrequent in Newman's letters. In the *Letter to Jelf* written in defence of Tract 90, Newman claims to be blood-brother to Scott, Coleridge, and Wordsworth. He had certainly read more of Coleridge than he wished others to know (LD IV, pp. 256, 289; V, p. 53); see the splendid anecdote in Harold Anson, *Looking Forward* (1968), p. 63, recording Newman's saying to Acland that he could not read Coleridge because he did not live with Mrs Coleridge. (In general see H F Davis in *Dublin Review* 435 (1945), pp. 165–73.)

15. *Remains* II, pp. 383–411 = Tract 63. Newman in LD VI, p. 226; VM II, pp. 217f.

16. *Rem.* I, p. 336.

17. See Froude's letter to Newman of 4 March 1835 in LD V, p. 68; also *Remains* I, p. 363 of 8 April 1834. The same principle for interpreting the Articles is stated in Keble's sermon on Tradition (1836). It was an accepted Tractarian axiom substantially before Tract 90. Panic led the Hebdomadal Board to invite Convocation to approve a declaration that the Articles are to be subscribed in their original sense and in that 'now to be proposed'.

18. LD VI, p. 18.

19. PPS I, p. 20, echoing Augustine, *Soliloquia*, i, 2, 7.

20. LD V, p. 40, March 1835.

21. VM II, p. 236. LD XXI, pp. 13–14 of 8 January 1864 records that, as an Anglican, Newman felt Protestants to be lax on purity. In Rome in 1847 he found the people unquestioning in faith, but dishonest (and dirty): 'They have not that *living* faith which leads to . . . sanctity' (LD XII, p. 24).

22. While Newman (according to the *Apologia*) looked back on this sermon, heard on the Sunday after his return from Sicily where he had nearly died, as the starting-point of the Oxford Movement, Isaac Williams (*Autobiography*, pp. 95–6) records that in the opinion of most people the sermon was 'indiscreet and fruitless'. The resemblance of Keble's character (hatred of humbug, playfulness, oddity, sensitivity to others, and severity) to that of St Philip Neri was among the factors leading Newman to become an Oratorian (LD XII, p. 25).
23. Letter to Faussett of 1838, VM II, p. 210.
24. LD VI, p. 61. All statements of a Via Media tend to become negative by stressing what is not to be said rather than what is.
25. VM I, p. 83.
26. Pusey (*Letter to the Bishop of Oxford*, 1839, p. 136) thought 'the miserable state of Roman Catholic countries' a consequence of withholding the cup from the laity.
27. Newman liked the statement of the (anti-Roman) Joseph Hall (1574–1656), bishop of Norwich: 'O blessed Mary, he cannot bless thee, he cannot honour thee too much, that deifies thee not' (cited in LD XXI, p. 34, a letter of 1 February 1864). He was careful never to read *The Glories of Mary* by St Alfonso Liguori (*Diff. Angl.* II, p. 98).

   The *Essay on Development* of 1845 sought to turn the edge of the Anglican arguments that late medieval centralization in the papal monarchy had left Anglicans more closely continuous with the ancient patristic Church than Rome, and the apostolic succession, even without universality of communion, was a sufficient guarantee of authenticity (cf. LD XI, p. 28).
28. Edward Norman, *The English Catholic Church in the Nineteenth Century* (Oxford 1984), p. 6.
29. The printed sermons sold well, and provided Newman with a steady income. Keble told Newman that reading them was 'the next thing to talking with you' (*Keble Corresp.* 1917, p. 217). The re-editing of PPS by W J Copeland (1868), who remained Anglican, led Newman to reissue his other Anglican works (LD XXVI, p. 293).
30. LD V, p. 32. (The letter is dated 27 February 1835.)
31. e.g. PPS I, pp. 32 ff. on those who admire biblical prose, though it contains much they themselves would not have said but which is suitable for the lower classes; or V, p. 42, 'A man of literature is considered to preserve his dignity by doing nothing.'
32. PPS III, p. 195.
33. *Diff. Angl.* I, p. 7; cf. PPS II, p. 289. The conclusion is not as compelling as Newman thought. Archbishop John Bird Sumner who gave this answer would have been regarded as heretical by a high Anglican for so speaking (so LD XII, p. 204; cf. XXV, p. 429). A heretical or ill-instructed archbishop no more speaks authoritatively for the Anglican communion than a similarly disqualified pope, such as Honorius (condemned by the Sixth Ecumenical Council for heresy),

on behalf of the Roman see. Newman can suggest that even a heretical pope, when speaking *ex cathedra*, could be protected from error as much as Balaam or Caiaphas (LD XXV, pp. 355f, of 10 July 1871). This reflects less a confidence in papal inerrancy than a faith that the universal Church will not be misled when not quite correctly instructed by bishops.

34. See, for example, on the Church PPS III, pp. 190ff., 206ff.; apostolic succession II, p. 401; IV, pp. 174ff.; priesthood II, pp. 300ff.; baptism II, p. 93 etc.; Eucharist II, p. 249; IV, p. 147; VI, pp. 136–141; frequent communion V, p. 28. A poetic passage on the sacraments in V, pp. 10–11; Immaculate Conception of BVM in II, p. 132.

35. PPS, IV, p. 36.

36. ibid., IV, p. 138.

37. ibid., VI, p. 108.

38. ibid., V, p. 183.

39. ibid., VI, p. 307.

40. ibid., VI, p. 80, esp. IV, pp. 12–13.

41. ibid., III, p. 13.

42. ibid., IV, p. 160.

43. ibid., V, pp. 288ff., 337.

44. ibid., V, p. 350.

45. See, for example, PPS V, pp. 288ff., 337; also polemically anti-Anglican statement in LD XII, p. 273 written in 1848 (the Anglican clergyman is gentleman, scholar, kindhearted father of the family, no saint). Denunciations of worldliness drew Anglican congregations at St Mary's; they were not well received in Rome in 1847 (LD XII, p. 13), where a critique of worldly Catholics was resented.

46. The custom was a consequence of requiring communicants for a celebration. A number of parish churches celebrated the Communion quarterly. Newman introduced an early communion each Sunday at St Mary's in 1837.

    A letter of 1864 records that the wine customarily used for Anglican Communion services was called (ironically enough) 'Trent', and was laced with brandy, treacle and raspberry vinegar, so that it was unpleasant unless diluted with water (LD XXI, p. 77). This report goes strangely with Newman's hostile accounts of Anglican Communion services at which the remains of the wine were the excuse for a merry and profane party in the vestry afterwards (LD XII, p. 293 and elsewhere), such a scandal being treated as typical and characteristic.

47. PPS III, p. 310; VI, p. 188.

48. LD VI, pp. 42, 125. Anglo-Catholic borrowing of Roman ceremonial later seemed to Newman sectarian (LD XII, p. 157 of 19 January 1848).

49. LD VI, p. 89 of 1837.

50. LD VI, p. 139. On the Laudian custom of bowing at Jesus' name, PPS V, p. 19.

51. Ward's book, *The Ideal of a Christian Church* (1844), claimed the right to hold and teach every article of Roman Catholic faith and devotional practice and yet to remain in the Church of England. The ingenuity of the argument provoked anger. In February 1845 he was censured and deprived of his degree (given on the assumption that the recipient accepted the Thirty-Nine Articles); but at the same occasion in the Sheldonian a censure of Tract 90 was vetoed by the Proctors, evidently on the ground that Tract 90 expressed a legitimate position where Ward's book did not. Newman expressed gratitude, even though by that date his confidence in the Church of England had evaporated.

52. See the letter to the lawyer, E L Badeley, of 23 August 1844, printed in *Keble Corresp.* 1917, p. 327. On the incomprehensibility to Newman of Pusey's remaining an Anglican see the striking letter to Catherine Ward of 25 September 1848 (LD XII, pp. 268–75), cataloguing the Protestantisms of seventeenth century Laudians. Perhaps he did not believe in the Real Presence (LD XIII, p. 455)?

53. See Thirlwall's *Charges* I (*Remains literary and theological*, ed. J J S Perowne, 1877), pp. 1–52. Thirlwall regarded the controversy about justification as one of words, involving no real difference of opinion; that about Scripture and tradition as more theoretical than actual; apostolic succession 'has been held by a large part of our best divines'. Newman's treatment of Article 22 could not be supported; but a denial of the general legitimacy of his position would be wrong. Thirlwall's *Charge* of 1848 (ibid., pp. 99–140) is a frontal attack on the *Essay on Development*, sharing J B Mozley's judgement that the presuppositions of that book are deeply sceptical. Newman was grateful for the *Charge* of 1842, offended by that of 1848 (LD XXVI, p. 235).

54. *Discussions and Arguments*, p. 343: 'England . . . the paradise of little men, the purgatory of great ones.' On Newman's long agony see above n. 3.

55. This question had disturbed him since Wiseman's article in the *Dublin Review*, quoting Augustine's triumphant sentence refuting the Donatist claim to be the sole survival of the true Church, the rest of Christendom outside N. Africa being polluted: *Securus iudicat orbis terrarum* — 'the world judges that without the least anxiety'. The requirement of universality put a question mark against Anglicanism without vindicating Roman claims to be its embodiment. The argument's force was of course great if one believed the papacy to be occupied by Antichrist. And if one did not so believe, it became a question whether the separation of the sixteenth century could be justified.

56. LD XXVII, p. 138. Roman refusal to accept the validity of Anglican Orders (which Newman came to think doubtful) has tended to obscure the fact that far more vehement attacks came from Puritans who found Cranmer's Ordinal indistinguishable from the Pontifical.

57. Newman admired and liked Acton personally, and thought the excommunication of Döllinger cruel; but he did not share their

difficulties with *Pastor aeternus*. No doubt that was not only because he had long held to the infallibility of the Church and to the propriety of seeing the pope as the organ and voice of decision in teaching authority, but also because he held that the interpretation of an *ex cathedra* utterance depends upon long study by the *Schola theologorum* and upon the sense in which it is ultimately received by the faithful. Newman did not envisage instant, unreflecting acceptance. The truth of a definition should be 'manifest', as stated in the ARCIC I *Final Report* A II 29, p. 95 (a text surprisingly criticized by the Congregation for the Doctrine of the Faith since the same doctrine is in the 1983 Code of Canon Law, 749, 3).

58. See the texts printed in Cuthbert Butler's *Life of Bishop Ullathorne*, II, pp. 101–5, and in LD XXVII, pp. 401–11. It is part of the paradox of Newman that the view of the magisterium which converted him to Roman Catholicism was utterly uncongenial at Rome. He understood authority to lie in what Ian Ker has called a creative interplay between the magisterium and private judgement (*John Henry Newman: A Biography*, 1988, p. 523, quoting LD XX, pp. 425–6).

59. E Burke, *Speech on the Acts of Uniformity* (1772).

· 4 ·

Newman's Significance for the Roman Catholic Church

ERIC D'ARCY

As noted in the Introduction, Newman's influence on his adopted communion, though profound, has been a chequered one. Though such suspicions and hostility as existed during his lifetime were to recede when he was made a cardinal in 1879, his writings became a renewed source of controversy not long after his death because of Modernists such as Loisy and Tyrrell (who were subsequently condemned by the Vatican) laying claim to him as their source of inspiration. The Second Vatican Council (1962–5), however, set the official seal of approval on many of Newman's leading ideas, and it is for this reason that it is often named 'Newman's Council'. Even before that Council Dr D'Arcy was already well known as an academic concerned with exploring the implications of Newman's thought, as reflected in his book Conscience and its Right to Freedom *(1961). Now an archbishop, he shows commendable pastoral concern in what follows. Rather than looking to the past, he takes an issue of immediate concern – the Church's desire to produce a new catechism, a fresh exposition of its doctrines for the purposes of teaching – and illustrates how effectively Newman's thought can be used as the best guide in this major task. Readers should not, however, be misled into supposing that a point of merely transitory significance is being made. In effect the new Catechism is being used as a test case of how religious truth should be communicated in the modern world, and Newman is offered as our guide.*

Newman makes a strong distinction between, on the one hand, exactitude in secular scholarship, and, on the other,

> that true religious zeal which leads theologians to keep the sacred Ark of the Covenant in every letter of its dogma, as a tremendous deposit for which they are responsible. In this curious sceptical world, such sensitiveness is the only human means by which the treasure of faith can be kept inviolate.[1]

But Newman also says:

> There is no greater mistake, surely, than to suppose that a revealed truth precludes originality in the treatment of it . . . [The] re-assertion of what is old with a luminousness of explanation which is new, is a gift inferior only to that of revelation itself.[2]

There is obviously tension between these two claims. I open with them, not as an epigraph to academic exegesis of Newman's writings, to see whether he succeeds in resolving the tension, but as entry for exploring the practical, pastoral, possibilities of a new specific significance of Newman for Roman Catholics in the 1990s. I suggest that he can help us capitalize to the full on the providential opportunity opening out to us with the coming of the Catechism for the Universal Church. In 1991 Roman Catholic religious education-ists will be finding themselves entrusted with a responsibility unprecedented in our history. It will involve them in full-blooded and simultaneous fidelity to *both* those ideals of Newman – as if one were not difficult enough.

Just twenty years after the end of the Second Vatican Council, an Extraordinary Synod was held in Rome. It ran from October to December 1985, and gathered bishop-representatives of nearly every Catholic hierarchy in the world. Pope John Paul was present in person at plenary sessions. At the end of the wide-ranging programme the Synod unanimously requested 'a universal catechism or compendium of all the Church's doctrines, both on faith and morals'. The Holy Father promptly acquiesced in the request, and soon afterwards set up a Commission to see to it.

By November 1989 they had completed and printed a Provisional Text of what is to be called a 'Catechism for the Universal Church' (CUC). Then, in accordance with the pope's wishes, began a process of consultation with the entire Catholic Episcopate. Every bishop in the world was sent a copy and each of us was invited to send within seven months our 'observations, suggestions and proposals' on the provisional text, for 'the utmost consideration in preparing the Definitive Version'.

The first thing to emphasize is this: no matter how perfectly that Definitive Version fulfils the aspirations held for it, this is only the end of Stage One: Stage One of the two-stage process envisaged by the Extraordinary Synod. The Synod Fathers stipulated 'a universal catechism or compendium of the Church's doctrines, both on faith and morals, to serve as a reference-point for the catechisms and compendia being produced in various areas'. When Pope John Paul consented so promptly to their request, he repeated this statement of intent.

It will certainly not be enough, therefore, simply to publish the English-language version of the Definitive Text, no matter how accurate, elegant and vigorous the English, no matter how attractive the illustrations, or how beautiful the whole production. The CUC itself has never been intended for a classroom text. However satisfactory the outcome of the initiative taken and eventually concluded by the Universal Church, that will still be only the end of Stage One.

Stage Two will consist in preparing and publishing the many national and catechetical texts required, and all the resources they in turn will entail. This will be just as important as Stage One – and, before God, a great honour to every faithful person called to take part in it. The Papal Commission itself said that the CUC is addressed to 'those responsible for the preparation and approval of texts based on it'. Every such participant will be entitled to perceive in all humility a personal reference in Eucharist Prayer I's petition for 'those who hold and teach the Catholic faith that comes to us from the Apostles'.

Nevertheless, however privileged the task may be, in the English-speaking world at least it bristles with difficulties. I believe that Newman can contribute significantly to resolving three of them. Let me start with the one which many of my own friends, active in religious education, find particularly disturbing.

I

The idea 'that belief belongs to the mere intellect, not to the heart also' is anathema to Newman; he sees it as part of the 'principle of philosophies and heresies, which is very weakness'.[3] This conviction is central to his notion of how the faith is to be taught.

> The heart is commonly reached, not through the reason, but through the imagination, by means of direct impressions, by the testimony of facts and events, by history, by description. Persons influence us, voices melt us, looks subdue us, deeds inflame us. Many a man will live and die upon a dogma: no man will be a martyr for a conclusion.[4]

This is an equally passionate conviction with the mainstream of religious educationists today. Indeed, many of them are wary about a strongly doctrinal approach to the life of faith. They suspect that in practice such an approach will mean a lapse into an impersonal, head-without-heart catechetic, unrelated to experience. It seems providential therefore that the Newman centenary occurs at the very time when they are bracing themselves to deal with the CUC. A deep and growing fellow-feeling with Newman will steadily accumulate both a sense of companionship with his remarkable personality, and provide concrete guidance in many moments of awkward decision.

To begin with, let us take his approach in principle; and then look at his own two most devastating personal experiences.

Many fear today that an objectivist view of faith will lead to regimented, rationalistic uniformity in the life of faith. Newman, however, was conscious of the obverse difficulty: that recognition of the individual and personal character of faith would lead to accusations of subjectivism, relativism, 'private judgementism' and the like. He therefore proposes as starting-point a quotation from an impeccably objectivist Roman theologian, Giovanni Perrone, his own old professor at Propaganda College: 'The *motivum credibilitatis* is personal to each individual.' This is diplomatically chosen, and Newman proceeds to develop it:

> Such individual conviction . . . is *sui generis* and varies with the individual . . . faith must rest on reason, nay even in the case of children and of the most ignorant and dull peasant, wherever faith is living and loving . . . [But] the faith and reason of which I speak are subjective, private, personal and unscientific . . .[5]

As so often, Newman spends little time on developing a theory for reconciling *prima facie* inconsistency between positions, if he is quite sure that each is true. The practice is certainly telling in this case; and many of the religious educationists whom I have mentioned will find themselves empathizing readily in the two most intensely personal experiences of his faith-journey. It cannot escape them that each occurred while he was immersed in explicitly doctrinal work.

There is a hierarchy of doctrinal truths, and in the late 1830s he had been especially concerned with what in England had just come to be called ecclesiology. He had been embroiled in controversy over his own theory of the Church of England as the Via Media – midway, that is, between the extremes of Protestantism on one side, and Romanism on the other.

In the summer of 1839 he was able to turn from strife and agitation, and set to quiet research into one of the two supreme members of that hierarchy of truths: the incarnation itself. The only person in residence at Oriel, he turned back at last to studying the turbulent history of the fourth and fifth centuries when the Fathers of the Church and their allies, both religious and political, had hammered out the classical dogmas of the origin and nature of Jesus Christ – 'the course of reading', he says, 'which years before I had chosen as especially my own'.[6] He was absorbed in the fifth century, on the way to finalizing publications to which he was committed.

> About the middle of June I began to study and master the history of Monophysites. I was absorbed in the doctrinal question . . . It was during this course of reading that for the first time a doubt came upon me of the tenableness of Anglicanism . . . The Church of the Via Media was in the position of the Oriental Communion; Rome was, where she now is; and the Protestants were the Eutycheans.[7]

Immersed in the research which was his métier – 'my stronghold was Antiquity' – he might have expected to be safe from the agitations of the day; but worse soon followed. Some friends put into his hands a *Dublin Review* article by Nicholas (later Cardinal) Wiseman on the 'Anglican Claim', which dealt with the Donatist schism of North Africa. Newman had long been familiar with this history, and at first saw nothing special in Wiseman's article; but his friend Robert Williams urged on his attention 'the palmary words of St Augustine, which were contained in one of the extracts made in the *Review*, and which had escaped my observation.

Securus iudicat orbis terrarum.'[8] Not only while Williams kept repeating them to him, but still after he had gone, they had an overwhelming effect. Telling as they were in the Donatist case, they told even more in the Monophysite. The words had an oracular, almost an incantatory, effect on him. Was his whole church criteriology misconceived? What price Via Media now? In his distress he wrote to a friend that he had 'had the first real hit from Romanism which has happened to me . . . I must confess it has given me a stomach-ache'.[9]

> After a while, I got calm, and at length the vivid impression upon my imagination passed away . . . [but I] had seen the shadow of a hand upon the wall . . . He who has seen a ghost, cannot be as if he had never seen it. The heavens had opened and closed again. The thought for the moment had been, 'The Church of Rome will be found right after all'; then it had vanished. My old convictions remained as before.[10]

Two summers later, by then having moved out to Littlemore, Newman was again relieved to turn to the peace and quiet of his study. Six months had passed since Tract 90 came out, and the atmosphere had been filled with the *Sturm und Drang* which it had provoked. With relief he returned to translating the Treatises of St Athanasius. At first this afforded the 'refuge' he had counted on. But soon the work itself confronted him with the first of the 'three blows which broke me'.

> I had got but a little way in my work, when my trouble returned on me. The ghost had come a second time. In the Arian history I found the very same phenomenon, in a far bolder shape, which I had found in the Monophysite. I had not observed it in 1832. Wonderful that this should come upon me! I had not sought it out; I was reading and writing in my own line of study, far from the controversies of the day, on what is called a 'metaphysical' subject; but I saw clearly, that in the history of Arianism, the pure Arians were the Protestants, the semi-Arians were the Anglicans, and that Rome now was what it was then.[11]

I am not concerned here with the argument which leapt from Christology in the fourth and fifth centuries to ecclesiology in the nineteenth. I am concerned to show that Newman's consternation over a doctrinal issue is a world away from an impersonal, head-without-heart attitude unrelated to experience, to which many religious educationists dread that a strongly doctrinal approach may lead.

Is this *bouleversement* of Newman very different from that of any academic suddenly confronted with the refutation of one link in a chain of reasoning essential to some work in hand? An instance familiar to every Oxford student of philosophy is Gottlob Frege's receipt of Russell's Paradox when the second volume of his *Grundgesetze* was already in the press: 'Hardly anything more unfortunate can befall a scientific writer than to have one of the foundations of his edifice shaken after the work is finished.'[12] Is this all that happened in Newman's case? Surely not. For Frege it simply meant: back to the drawing-board; he added an Appendix, trying to patch the damage. For Newman it was something more like an opthalmologist who finds from an X-ray of his own eye that it will have to be removed.

Hilaire Belloc, for one, appears to have viewed the significance of the great christological controversies in the fourth and fifth centuries as simply intellectual and cultural. He says that they served to establish the tradition of intellectual vitality as a normal part of Christian life. More specifically Belloc believed that those controversies occurred at a period of cultural staleness and fatigue; and that they

> revitalised the dying fourth and fifth centuries . . . [They] gave new life. If you read the literature of the time you see that all was tired out, *except* this new interest. Nothing could have saved the excellence of sculpture, architecture and letters: they had gone long before . . . But the power to revive was saved. It was like a belated love-affair saving a man from drink.[13]

Those controversies often descended into mere populist dillettantism, such as we see in St Gregory of Nyssa's delicious snapshot of Constantinople. The great cities of Eastern Christianity were convulsed by the questions. What was the nature and origin of Jesus? Was he simply *made by* God, the first and greatest of creatures, but *created* nonetheless? Or was he eternally *begotten of* the Father, perfectly his equal in every way? With tart amusement Gregory recalls how acutely *engagé* in all this was *le tout Constantinople* when he arrived there. He had found the city full of labourers and slaves who are all profound theologians . . . You ask a money-changer the day's exchange rate for silver; his reply is to give you a disquisition on *begotten, not made.* You ask a baker for a loaf of bread; he tells you that the Son is inferior to the Father. You go to the hot-baths and ask the attendant if your bath is ready; his answer is that the Son was *created out of nothing.*[14]

Newman believed strongly in the intrinsic value of intellectual and cultural life; it was not, for him, simply a means to religious ends. *The Idea of a University*, and a dozen other places in his writings, make this abundantly clear. But he would be disappointed that Belloc should see nothing but intellectual and cultural values in those great conflicts over doctrinal truth.

No doubt he enjoyed Gregory's caricature. But when he was a curate in St Clement's pastoring Anglicans, when he was an Oratorian in Birmingham pastoring Catholics, he would never have been content to make those parishes into replicas of the city which Gregory depicts.

Newman is playing for infinitely higher stakes. Church doctrines, the truths of the Christian faith, are not just the insights of some consummate religious genius achieved, say, by extracting undreamt-of vistas of implication from Aristotle's concept of the Prime Mover eternally contemplating its own perfection. Church doctrines, for Newman, develop from those things that Jesus had heard from his Father and confided to his friends, and entrusted to them to hand on to every man or woman who would ever come to believe in him.

They will rarely produce Richter-scale readings like those caused by the two apparitions of Newman's ghost. But, one way and another, more intimately than the spectacles we wear, they help determine the way that we see life: more like the way Friedrich Waismann argues that the structure of an individual's particular native language helps determine the way in which that individual perceives colour. No matter how learned one was in the history of dogma and academic theology, a doctrine which one could accurately recite but which made no difference to the way one experienced and lived life would be (to Newman's mind) rather like an accurate photograph of a beloved friend, instead of the actual person in the flesh.

II

Let us turn to Stage Two of the process envisaged by the Extraordinary Synod, by the Holy Father, and by the Commission he set up. In Stage Two the CUC is to be 'a Magisterial text, serving as a point of reference for national and diocesan catechisms', and 'addressed to those responsible for their composition and approval'. I shall concentrate on texts and resources designed for senior high-school students. Newman said: 'I want a laity . . . who know their religion, who enter into it, who know just where they stand, who know what they hold, and what they do not, who know their Creed well and can give an account of it.'[15] In his day that was an impossible dream. He himself admitted in the next breath that it seemed 'severe and exorbitant'. He was addressing the Brothers of the Oratory, a handful of disciples. Throughout the English-speaking world, at that time, few Catholics had a high-school education, and even fewer teachers existed who could carry through such an ambitious programme. What was then a dream is today, in God's providence, normal bread-and-butter reality. In English-speaking countries of the First World at least, thousands upon thousands of young Catholics quite normally complete thirteen years of formal full-time schooling, right to the top of senior high-school. Dozens and dozens of Catholic Teacher Colleges or Faculties of Education enjoy equal recognition with their non-Catholic and secular peers. In many places they are government-funded; in many others, diocesan Education Offices lay on special courses in Theology, Scripture and Catechetics for Catholic teachers who graduated in non-Catholic Colleges.

And now, *ad diem talem carpendum*, the Universal Church provides the CUC: a single-volume, uniquely authoritative, doctrinal data-bank for those who must prepare the culture-specific texts and resources for us to seize this providential opportunity. What will we need them to provide?

Any actual catechetical text, to be successful, will have to be composed according to the very best available educational models, principles and techniques. It will have to be accurately pitched for the developmental stage of its particular intended readership. In addition, it must also satisfy simultaneously two other requirements, demanded specifically by the task in hand:

(1) It must convey the doctrinal content of the *Catechism for the Universal Church* without departing or derogating from it by one jot or tittle.

(2) It must render that doctrinal content in the style and idiom of contemporary anglophone culture.

This is a tall order. Newman will be a constant source, of guidance certainly, but of companionship and encouragement as well. He would not have been especially surprised to find that peer-pressure has built up against requirement (1). It is worth dwelling on the utterly fundamental importance he attached to that issue.

In the spring of 1879, thirty-two years after being ordained in Rome, Newman went back there to be made a Cardinal. The *Biglietto* – formal notification that Pope Leo XIII had designated him in secret consistory – was ceremonially brought to him at the Palazzo della Pigna, where the English Cardinal Howard had invited him to use his own *salone* for the occasion. A jubilant group had gathered there, and Newman delivered the celebrated address which came to be known as the Biglietto Speech. During it he said:

> In a long course of years I have made many mistakes. I have nothing of that high perfection which belongs to the writings of saints . . . But, I rejoice to say, to one great mischief I have from the first opposed myself. For thirty, forty, fifty years I have resisted to the best of my powers the spirit of Liberalism in religion. Never did Holy Church need champions against it more sorely than now when, alas! it is an error overspreading, as a snare, the whole earth . . . Liberalism in religion is that doctrine that there is no positive truth in religion, but that one creed is as good as another. This is the teaching which is gaining force and substance daily. It is inconsistent with any recognition of religion as *true*. It teaches that . . . Revealed religion is not a truth, but a sentiment and a taste: not an objective fact . . .[16]

'Thirty, forty, fifty years' is interesting. Fifty, and forty, years before this Newman was an Anglican; and it is quite plainly on the record that he was then indeed fighting the good fight against doctrinal indifferentism (as we would call 'Liberalism in religion').

It is a fashion of the day to suppose that all insisting on precise Articles of Faith is injurious to the cause of spiritual religion, and inconsistent with an enlightened view of it; that it is all one to maintain, that the Gospel requires the reception of definite and positive Articles, and to acknowledge it to be technical and formal; that such a notion is superstitious, and interferes with the liberty wherewith Christ has set us free; that it argues a deficient insight into the principles and ends, a narrow comprehension of the spirit of His Revelation.[17]

He made the positive point emphatically, preaching as an Anglican on our Lord's ascension and his sending the Holy Spirit:

What are the deep and hidden reasons why Christ went and the Spirit came? Marvellous and glorious beyond our understanding! Let us worship in silence; meanwhile, let us jealously maintain this and every other portion of our Creed, lest, by dropping jot or tittle, we suffer truths contained therein to escape us.[18]

Strongest of all, both about our privilege and our responsibility, are the words of Newman with which my article opened. While esteeming precision in trades or in secular scholarship, he distinguishes it strongly from

that true religious zeal which leads theologians to keep the sacred Ark of the Covenant in every letter of its dogma, as a tremendous deposit for which they are responsible. In this curious sceptical world, such sensitiveness is the only human means by which the treasure of faith can be kept inviolate.[19]

If true for theologians, how much more so for those who plan and write and publish catechetical texts for Christ's young!

It is hardly surprising to find such support in Newman for requirement (1). It is the story of his life, up to and beyond the Biglietto Speech, well into his eighties. But what would he have thought of Requirement (2) – that the substance of the CUC must, without loss of doctrinal content, be rendered in our cultural style and idiom?

This is no easy task, even when simply translating a contemporary foreign text into our own vernacular – I have seen the Italian *sensibile* routinely translated as 'sensible', and *superbo* as 'superb'. The religious educationist's task is far more difficult: to write in our cultural style and idiom, with no loss of doctrinal content. This is notoriously tricky. I once heard a lecturer tell a seminar of Religious

Education teachers and catechists that we must eliminate 'the whole notion of redemption, ransom, and all their ramifications' from our preaching, teaching and catechesis because it is 'meaningless to the modern mind'. Yet the very word had just then been given dreadful new currency by terrorists holding hostage an aircraft full of passengers and bargaining by radio-telephone for their release in exchange for an acceptable *ransom*.

Newman was far more alert to the problems at issue. Stephen Prickett has argued: 'There is no doubt that Newman's was the most subtle, the most satisfying, and the most comprehensive solution to the problem of the relationship of the religious to the poetic that the nineteenth century was to see.'[20] On one related issue Prickett, not altogether perhaps without tongue in cheek, finds that 'somewhat unexpectedly, Roland Barthes and Newman join hands'.[21] At all events, on the practical problem of producing national catechetical texts which transmit the doctrinal content of the CUC, Newman is a strongly committed supporter of requirement (2). *Tempore non suspecto*, when he was really counter-attacking some Utramontanist English Catholics who had been impugning his Catholic orthodoxy and fidelity, Newman wrote:

> And certainly, if there is one consideration more than another which should make us English grateful to Pope Pius the Ninth, it is that, by giving us a Church of our own, he has prepared the way for our own habits of mind, our own manner of reasoning, our own tastes, and our own virtues, finding a place and thereby a sanctification, in the Catholic Church.[22]

Newman was no chauvinist, no jingoist – think of his forthright answer to Gerard Manley Hopkins' 'appalling' letter about the Irish Patriots; Newman wrote, 'If I were an Irishman, I should be (in heart) a rebel.' He certainly does not think it is only English Catholics who should be allowed their own manner of reasoning, and tastes, and virtues: theirs is only one application of a general principle.

> Again, if Christianity be a universal religion, suited not simply to one locality or period, but to all times and places, it cannot but vary in its relationships and dealings with the world around it, that is, it will develop. Principles require a very various application according as persons and circumstances vary, and must be thrown

into new shapes according to the form of society which they are to serve.[23]

This is as integral to Newman's thought about doctrinal preaching and teaching as it is to that of any religious educationist today. How far will he take it?

> There is no greater mistake, surely, than to suppose that a revealed truth precludes originality in the treatment of it . . . This faculty of investing with associations, of applying to particular purposes, of impressing upon the imagination, is creative . . . And so in like manner with Scripture; to enter into the mind of the sacred author, to follow his train of thought, to bring together to one focus the lights which various parts of Scripture throw upon his text, and to give adequate expression to the thoughts thus evolved, in other words the breadth of view, the depth, or the richness, which we recognise in certain early expositions, is a creation . . . [In certain circumstances, the] re-assertion of what is old with a luminousness of explanation which is new, is a gift inferior only to that of revelation itself.[24]

Given the awe in which Newman holds revelation, could he say anything that would show more plainly how exalted a store he sets on authentic creativity in Catechetics?

III

Contemporary anglophone Religious Education needs a well-articulated account of the role of doctrine in faith. Newman sets out no account in the schematic style of a manual, even in the *Grammar* itself: but the components of one take stronger and deeper root as one reads him. Here again, there is cumulative, strengthening reassurance and conviction for anyone who once feared that a strongly doctrinal catechetic will mean an impersonal, head-without-heart approach unrelated to experience. Note the economy of a famous passage early in the *Apologia*.

> When I was 15, (in the autumn of 1816), a great change of thought took place in me. I fell under the influences of a definite Creed, and received into my intellect impressions of dogma, which, through God's mercy, have never been effaced or obscured.[25]

'Received into my intellect impressions of dogma' is a densely laden phrase.

First, *received:* one does not arrive at faith by excogitation, by dint of one's brain-power or industry. One receives it *ab Alio*: it has to be given to one.

> 'Those things which thou hast heard from me through many witnesses', says St Paul to Timothy, 'commit these same to faithful men, who shall be able to teach others also.' This body of truth was in consequence called the 'depositum', as being a substantive teaching, not a mere accidental deduction from Scripture. Thus St Paul says to his disciple and successor Timothy, 'Keep the deposit', 'hold fast the form of sound words', 'guard the noble deposit'. This important principle is forcibly insisted on by Irenaeus and Tertullian before the Nicene era, and by Vincent after it. 'O Timothy', says Vincent, 'guard the *depositum*, avoiding profane novelties of words.' Who is Timothy today? Who but the universal Church, or the whole body of prelates, whose duty it is both themselves to have the full knowledge of religion, and to instruct others in it? What means 'guard'? Guard the deposit because of enemies, lest, while men sleep, they sow tares upon the good seed, which the Son of Man has sowed in his field. What is 'the deposit'? That which has been entrusted to you, not which thou hast discovered; what thou hast received, not what thou hast thought out; a matter, not of cleverness, but of teaching; not of private handling, but of public tradition.[26]

The concept of the *depositum fidei* has been suffering an eclipse in the education of future English-speaking priests, teachers and catechists. St Paul's word *paratheke* was translated by the substantive *depositum* in the old Vulgate, and in the 1986 *Nova Vulgata Editio*; and by the substantive *dépôt* in the *Bible de Jérusalem*, which remarks in a footnote, '*Le dépôt de la foi: une des idées dominantes des Pastorales.*' There is a special entry *dépôt*, with cross-references to *enseigner* and *tradition*, in Léon-Dufour's *Dictionnaire du Nouveau Testament*. In most English translations, however, St Paul's substantive *paratheke* is rendered by some participial phrase. This is no doubt one reason for the disappearance of the term 'the deposit of the faith' from so much of the theology taught to future priests and future Catholic teachers. It is a real loss. Appreciation of the Church's patrimony in architecture, in the visual arts, and in music, waxes strong; but that of her doctrinal patrimony has waned.

Thanks however to the various centenary celebrations, many religious educationists will have had their appetite whetted for more about the nature and significance of the *depositum fidei* itself by reading and hearing what it meant to Newman.

Edward Hawkins was not one of Newman's life-long heroes. Newman soon came to regret that he had voted for Hawkins, rather than Keble, for Provost of Oriel. But Newman readily acknowledged the debt he owed Hawkins for a sermon on Tradition which had urged that the Bible 'was never intended to teach doctrine, but only to prove it; if we would learn doctrine, we must have recourse to the formularies of the Church; for instance to the Catechism, and to the Creeds'.[27] From this, and a dozen more nuanced sources, Newman developed his rich account of the *depositum fidei*. Some such account is presupposed by page after page of the CUC. It is one of the reasons for Newman's saying that at the age of fifteen he *received* impressions of dogma.

Secondly let us look briefly at the term *impressions* in that loaded phrase, 'I received into my intellect impressions of dogma'. The term carries no suggestion of vagueness, of judging or reporting 'impressionistically'. Newman adapted the term from David Hume, making it into a semi-technical term for his own purposes. In Hume's epistemology a primary distinction is made between 'impressions' and 'ideas'. Impressions, for Hume, are 'sensations, passions, and emotions as they make their first appearance in the soul'; ideas are the faint images of these in thinking and reason. Impressions are defined by Hume as 'those perceptions which enter the human mind with most force and violence'. Newman is not simply taking over Hume's theory. For Hume, impressions come via the senses and are registered in the affective powers; but for Newman it is the intellect on which is impressed, which receives impressions of, dogma. Newman is thus driving home the intimate role played in his life by dogma, as distinct from that played by the ideas of abstract reason.

The term 'impressions in the intellect' is something like Shakespeare's 'puzzles the will'. They both cross category-lines. 'Puzzlement' normally concerns the cognitive powers; Hamlet makes us feel the painfulness of indecision by applying it to the conative powers. Where 'impressions' in Hume are received in the affective powers, Newman makes us feel the profundity of the change that occurred in his religious life when he was fifteen, by saying that what his intellect received were impressions of dogma.

Third, we shall take the term *dogma* and leave 'intellect' until last. The strong impressions Newman received in that watershed autumn of 1816, he says, were 'impressions of dogma'. Lest you suspect that this *locus classicus* may really be just some *obiter dictum* tossed off early in the *Apologia*, let me quote words nearer a climax of the book:

> From the age of 15, dogma has been the fundamental principle of my religion: I know no other religion: I cannot enter into the idea of any other sort of religion . . . What I held in 1816, I held in 1833, and I hold in 1864. Please God, I shall hold it to the end.[28]

And so he did. From that moment in his mid-teens when he 'came under the influences of a definite Creed', this is everywhere in his thought, and he is deeply troubled at the spread of the very opposite influence:

> The most religiously-minded men are nowadays ready to give up important doctrinal truths because they do not understand their value. A cry is raised that the Creeds are unnecessarily minute, and even many who would defend them, through ignorance cannot.[29]

This is very close to the bone for us who worry over the doctrinal education of senior high school Catholics today. Hence the enthusiasm to give religious educationists every support in their task of taking full advantage of the opportunity presented by the CUC. But the ethos, the mores, the cultural climate in which their students live and learn and grow is enormously different from that of England in the year after Waterloo. The difficulties of presenting the Church's doctrines, in texts and curricula and resources that are truly efficacious, are far more resistant and multiplex now than then. Yet if the enterprise succeeds, especially at senior high school level, it will empower thousands upon thousands of young Catholic adults every year to discover for themselves that the doctrinal infrastructure of the faith is just as intellectually serious, just as well grounded and articulated, and just as thoroughly incarnate in contemporary culture, as are the other things they study.

This means, of course, that education-in-faith must involve the *intellect*, as well as the other powers connected with faith. So finally a word about this term, in that charged phrase of Newman, 'I received in my intellect impressions of dogma.' This too is crucial in Newman's account of faith. It has nothing to do with being an intellectual, or suggesting that real faith is the preserve of an educated élite. As he preached in one of his sermons, 'Gospel faith is what even the humblest member of the Church may and must contend for.' In the papers on faith and certainty he is intensely interested in what count as good reasons for Christian believing for a factory girl, or a working man, or a washerwoman. In one of his 1860 notebooks he has one line marked NB: 'NB an accurate knowledge of the Catechism is a *motivum credibilitatis.*'[30]

But let me complete the sentence I began to quote from that sermon:

> This faith is what even the humblest member of the Church may and must contend for; and in proportion to his education will the circle of his knowledge enlarge . . . and, according as his power of grasping the sense of [the Creeds'] articles increases, so will it become his duty to contend for them in their fuller and more accurate form.[31]

Newman could not foresee the enormously increased number of Catholics going right through high school, a hundred years after his death; but he has foreseen very accurately their need for their intellect, along with their other capacities for faith, to be educated in the faith. Today's sixth-former needs a sixth-form initiation into theology, as much as a sixth-form initiation into geology or sociology; at a comparable level of intellectual sophistication and rigour. Collaboration between theologians and religious educationists is better developed today than ever before. The CUC will provide them with an unprecedented data-base.

Experience is certainly indispensable for making the truths of the faith one's own, for penetrating their significance, for interiorizing them at ever greater depth. This is true above all of experience by prayer: in the liturgy, in popular devotions, in private personal prayer and meditation. But in addition to these, one must have doctrinal input at a similar pedagogical level to the rest of one's high school education. A faith-development whose *cognitive* powers are deprived or retarded in comparison with the rest of one's development severely handicaps one's growing towards a full and confident Christian adulthood. Such development of the intellectual powers in the *credenda* of revelation Newman calls natural, excellent and necessary:

> It is natural, because the intellect is one of our highest faculties; excellent, because it is our duty to use our faculties to the full; necessary, because unless we apply our intellect to revealed truth rightly, others will exercise their minds upon it wrongly.[32]

He describes the process even more richly in the first three of the nine principles which he draws out of the doctrine of the incarnation:

> 1. The principle of *dogma*, that is, supernatural truths irrevocably committed to human language, imperfect because it is human, but definitive and necessary because given from above.
> 2. The principle of *faith*, which is the correlative of dogma, being the absolute acceptance of the divine Word with an internal assent, in opposition to the informations, if such, of sight and reason.
> 3. Faith, being an act of the intellect, opens a way for inquiry, comparison and inference, that is, for science in religion, in subservience to itself; this is the principle of *theology*.[33]

Blessed is the young Catholic whose final years at high school comprise an education embodying those principles!

> I wish you to enlarge your knowledge, to cultivate your reason, to get an insight into the relation of truth to truth, to learn to view things as they are, to understand how faith and reason stand to each other, what are the bases and principles of Catholicism . . .[34]

This again is Newman speaking to that handful of Brothers of the Oratory, most of them past their first youth. But how his heart would have leaped in gratitude to Providence could he have known of the numerous fresh young minds at the end of the century after his own, throughout the English-speaking countries of the First World, for whom that seems quite normal; and who are so taught by dedicated religious and lay teachers who are themselves tertiary-educated in Scripture, theology, and education. It would be silly for us to be smug about it; but it would be crass to underestimate it.

All the same, Newman will never let us treat such an opportunity as if it concerned just one more of the 'subjects' being studied.

> One aspect of revelation must not be allowed to exclude or to obscure another; and Christianity is dogmatical, devotional, practical all at once; it is exoteric and it is esoteric; it is indulgent, and strict, it is light and dark; it is love, and it is fear.[35]

Even at his most severely analytic, he will never let the role of *intellect* in faith be separated from that of *heart. Cor ad cor loquitur* was his motto as Cardinal; now, with exquisite appropriateness, Oriel has inscribed it in the little oratory of Newman recently once more disclosed to view behind the organ in the chapel; and it is on the wall of the Catholic chaplaincy in the Old Palace. Faith for Newman is always *personal*; a living faith involves an irreducibly person-to-person relationship with Jesus Christ. He loved the phrase in the middle of St Bernard's sermon on the Song of Solomon, *Jesus mel in ore, in aure melos, in corde iubilus* (honey in the mouth, a tune in the ear, joy in the heart). The Bible, says Newman,

> is the best book of meditations which can be, because it is divine. This is why we see such multitudes in France and Italy giving up religion altogether. They have not *impressed upon their hearts* the life of Our Lord and Saviour as given us in the Evangelists. They *believe merely with the intellect*, not with the heart. Argument may overset a mere assent of the reason, but not a faith founded in a personal love for the Object of Faith.[36]

In his critical notice of John Seeley's unexpectedly best-selling *Ecce Homo*, Newman remarks that Seeley 'seems to imagine that the faith of a Catholic is the mere profession of a formula': whereas in fact

> the very life of personal religion among Catholics lies in a knowledge of the Gospels. It is the character and conduct of our Lord, His words, His deeds, His sufferings, His work, which are the very food of our devotion and rule of our life. 'Behold the man', which this author feels to be an object novel enough to write a book about, has been the contemplation of Catholics from the first age when St Paul said, 'The life that I now live in the flesh, I live in the faith of the Son of God, who loved me, and delivered himself up for me.' What Catholics, what Church

doctors, as well as Apostles have ever lived on, is not any numbe
of theological canons or decrees but, we repeat, the Christ Himself
as He is represented in concrete existence in the Gospels.[37]

The head is not more native to the heart, the heart unto the head
than they are both to one another in Newman's conception of faith
they are organically united; each enlivens the other. Trying to
express how successfully this unity is maintained everywhere in
Newman, I found myself recalling Martin Seymour-Smith's remark
about Shakespeare's Sonnets. A critic might attempt to separate
those elements in the Sonnets which are cognitively meaningful
from those which are emotive; but Seymour-Smith finds that, even
when one takes lines which appear to be purely emotive, analysis
proves 'their intellectual precision to be as intense in its hardness as
their passion is intense in its heat'.[38] *Dictis dicendis*, the
corresponding thing holds for Newman's account of heart and
intellect, of the doctrinal and the personal, in an authentic life of
faith.

IV

Gladstone once said at a private dinner party that there had been
nothing like Newman's influence at its Oxford height 'since Abelard
lectured in Paris'.[39] It is still the case that, over and above
commanding a style which makes him so pleasurable to read,
Newman still, a hundred years on, exercises a charm that captivates
a great many people. This is an uncovenanted mercy. It is all very
well for pastors like me to enthuse over the possible results of a
Stage Two completed, disseminated, smoothly running: with young
Catholics coming out of senior high school educated, mind and
heart, in the doctrinal riches of the CUC. But it would be insensitive
to forget what the planning and preparation of national and diocesan
texts is going to cost those who must carry it through. It is a comfort
that in Newman many will find the leading ideas which they will
have to shape into specific programme, curriculum, and actual text,
presented with clarity, vigour and charm.

English charm. Of course, English charm is a special phenomenon.
It has resisted analysis, imitation, and parody; it has never been
successfully cloned. But whatever it is that constitutes that enviable
English quality, Newman had it in rare degree. Undergraduates

crowded St Mary the Virgin to hear him preach. Heads of Houses changed the dinner hour, desperate to keep their young men away from his sermons. Parishioners of St Clement's, Tractarian dons, Tractarian clergy in rectories all over England hung on his words. Then, after he became a Roman Catholic, the same charm – priestly, gospel charm, not some secular counterfeit – had the same sort of effect on the Catholic poor of Birmingham, fellow converts, hundreds of correspondents. From far beyond England, great numbers sent money in excess even of the enormous expenses he incurred in the Achilli trial. Today still, a river of people are captivated by the charm of his personality.

To be sure, much is due to the pleasure of his style – a supervenient pleasure, like Aristotle's bloom on the cheek of youth. But there is constant originality of substance too.

So perhaps it really is providential that Newman's centenary is being celebrated just as religious educationists are realizing with awe the magnitude of all that will be asked of them, come the Definitive Version of the CUC. Participating in this or that centenary occasion, many of them will sense how congenial a companion and partner he may be. Certainly, he has no do-it-yourself kit to offer them. He sets out no cut-and-dried solutions. He does not have all the answers. But what many of them will find encouraging and sustaining, if they will make his many, varied writings their staple auxiliary reading, is that he becomes an unfailing source of companionship, understanding and fellow-feeling. In their hard, hard work they will find such qualities of substance, strength and charm as testified by no biased English witness, but by a Scot, Muriel Spark:

> I have noticed that to those who have been attracted by Newman, his personality continues very much alive. It is one of his gifts. He is far less dead, to me, than many of my contemporaries; and less dead, even, than Socrates for whom, in the day-dreams of my young youth, I thought it would be lovely to lay down my life. Socrates, too, had the love of God at heart; like him, Newman was said to be a 'corrupter of youth'. It was by way of Newman that I turned Roman Catholic. Not all the beheaded martyrs of Christendom, the ecstatic nuns of Europe, the five proofs of Aquinas, or the pamphlets of my Catholic acquaintance, provided anything like the answers that Newman did.[40]

NOTES

References to Newman's works are to the uniform edition of 1868–81, published by Longmans, Green & Co., unless otherwise stated.

1. J H Newman, *On Consulting the Faithful in Matters of Doctrine*, ed. and introd. by John Coulson (London, Geoffrey Chapman, 1961), p. 61.
2. *Historical Sketches* II, pp. 475–6.
3. *Essay on the Development of Doctrine*, p. 358.
4. *Discussions and Arguments*, p. 293.
5. *Theological Papers of John Henry Newman on Faith and Certainty*, ed. H M de Achaval sj and J Derek Holmes (Oxford, Clarendon Press, 1976), p. 84.
6. *Apologia*, p. 114.
7. ibid.
8. idem., pp. 116–17.
9. To F. Rogers, cit. Ian Ker, *John Henry Newman: A Biography* (Oxford, Clarendon Press, 1988), p. 182.
10. *Apologia*, pp. 117–18.
11. ibid., p. 139.
12. ed. Peter Geach and Max Black, *Translations from the Philosophical Writings of Gottlob Frege* (Oxford, Basil Blackwell, 1960), p. 234.
13. cit. Robert Speaight, *The Life of Hilaire Belloc* (London, Hollis & Carter, 1957), p. 388.
14. St Gregory of Nyssa, *Oratio de deitate Filii et Spiritus Sancti*, Migne PG 46, 557B: my paraphrase.
15. *Lectures on the Present Position of Catholics in England*, pp. 372–3.
16. cit. Wilfrid Ward, *The Life of John Henry Cardinal Newman* (London, Longmans Green, 1912), vol. II, p. 460.
17. *Parochial & Plain Sermons* II, p. 259.
18. ibid., p. 213.
19. *On Consulting the Faithful*, p. 61.
20. Stephen Prickett, *Words and the Word* (Cambridge University Press, 1986), p. 68.
21. idem, p. 28.
22. *Apologia*, p. 269.
23. *Essay on Development of Doctrine*, p. 58.
24. *Historical Sketches* II, pp. 475–6.
25. *Apologia*, p. 4.
26. *Essays Critical and Historical* I, pp. 125–6.
27. *Apologia*, p. 9.
28. idem, p. 49.
29. cit. Ian Ker, p. 671.
30. *Theological Papers*, p. 90.

31. *Parochial & Plain Sermons* II, p. 256.
32. *Grammar of Assent*, p. 147.
33. *Essay on Development of Doctrine*, p. 325.
34. *Lectures on Present Position of Catholics in England*, p. 373.
35. *Essay on Development of Doctrine*, p. 36.
36. *Letters & Diaries* XXVI (Oxford, Clarendon Press), p. 87.
37. *Discussions & Arguments*, p. 387.
38. Martin Seymour-Smith, ed., *Shakespeare's Sonnets* (London, Heinemann, 1963), pp. 1–2.
39. cit. C S Dessain, *John Henry Newman* (London, Nelson, 1966), p. 43.
40. Muriel Spark, Foreword to Vincent Blehl sj, ed. and introd., *Realizations* (London, Darton, Longman & Todd, 1964), p. ix.

· 5 ·

Newman as a Philosopher of Religion

ANTHONY KENNY

Newman's reputation as a philosopher rests on two works, his University Sermons of 1843 and A Grammar of Assent of 1870. The latter in particular presents considerable difficulties for those unversed in philosophical issues. Readers have thus good reason to be grateful to a philosopher of Dr Kenny's distinction that, so far from using the opportunity to develop his own views, his contribution instead is mainly devoted to a careful exposition of the argument of these two works. The fact that Dr Kenny does this largely in Newman's own words should not be allowed to conceal from the reader the considerable efforts he has taken to give systematic form to Newman's essentially informal and discursive presentation. His contribution does, however, end with some briefly noted objections.

In the analytic tradition, which is dominant here and in much of the United States, the beginning of modern philosophy is often taken to be the writing, by Gottlob Frege, of an essay entitled *Begriffschrift* in 1879. In that essay, and in later writings, Frege made a great separation between logic and psychology, between the content of propositions on the one hand, and our mental acts about them on the other: he separated off the logical relations between propositions from the thoughts and images which might embody or accompany them. Frege made the distinction in order to concentrate not on the psychology but on the logic; he developed quantification theory, which is the kernel of modern symbolic logic; he defended a logicist theory of mathematics, and a realist theory of the philosophy of logic. Only rarely did he return to the topic of mental acts.

Ten years before the *Begriffschrift*, in the *Grammar of Assent*, Newman had made many of the same distinctions which Frege was to make, sometimes in the same terms, sometimes in different terms. Newman distinguished between the apprehension of a proposition and assent to a proposition, between the notional or logical content of a proposition and the realization of its content in the imagination. But whereas Frege disjoined logic from psychology in order to discard the psychology, Newman disjoined the two to downgrade the logic.

Unknown to Newman, the logic which he downgraded was in its last days. With *Begriffschrift*, Frege laid the ground for a new and much more versatile logic, based on quantification theory, which has developed from that day to this. The Aristotelian syllogistic which Newman sniffed at is now seen as only a small fragment of formal logic. But post-Frege logic, however expanded, and the philosophy of logic which deals with meaning, entailment, and formal proof, still needs to be supplemented, if we are to give a philosophical account of the human mind, with a theory of mental acts of the kind that Newman gave.

By 'psychology' Frege and Newman meant not the experimental science which now bears the name, but the philosophical study of psychological concepts which is nowadays called 'philosophy of mind' and the study of the nature and justification of human belief and knowledge which philosophers call 'epistemology'. From the time of Descartes until the nineteenth century epistemology was regarded by many as the central, foundational discipline of philosophy. Frege not only originated modern logic but started a school of philosophy which placed the theory of meaning – rather than epistemology – in the forefront of philosophical attention. Frege's successors followed him in this. Russell and the early Wittgenstein both propounded theories of belief, but they were theories of the logical structure of belief, not of its psychological nature or its epistemological justification. Frege in his logical symbolism had made room for an assertion sign: a sign corresponding to the mental act which is the main topic of Newman's *Grammar of Assent*. In his early *Tractatus logico-philosophicus* Wittgenstein criticized this: assertion belonged to psychology, not to logic.[1]

Newman and Frege, then, had a common starting point, the separation of logic from psychology, but Frege explored one side of the divided territory and Newman the other. Frege's work had a great progeny during the century after his essay. Newman's has had, among professional philosophers, almost none. But in recent decades professional philosophers in the analytic tradition have become interested in the topics which concerned him.

Wittgenstein's later philosophy took seriously topics which he had earlier dismissed. His notes of his last philosophical thoughts, written just before his death, began with an explicit reference to Newman. Having spent most of his life on theory of meaning Wittgenstein turned in his last years to the traditional problems of epistemology, seen from a new viewpoint. His posthumously published *On Certainty* covers many of the same topics as the *Grammar of Assent*, uses many of the same illustrations, and draws some of the same conclusions.

The most influential philosopher of religion in the analytic tradition at the present time, Alvin Plantinga of Notre Dame University, has devoted much of his best work to the question which is at the centre of Newman's book: How can religious belief be justified, given that the evidence for its conclusions seems so inadequate to the degree of its commitment?

Newman's own philosophical background is one that now seems alien to many. He was a philosopher in the British empiricist tradition. When he argues he argues with Locke and Hume. He was ill at ease, in his Catholic as well as his Anglican days, with scholastic philosophy. He was nominalistic in temper: 'Let units come first and (so-called) universals second; let universals minister to units, not units be sacrificed to universals.'[2] His theory of meaning, like that of the empiricists, is strongly imagist: it is the importance which he attaches to the imagination which is the driving force of his celebrated distinction between notional and real assent. Among twentieth-century professional philosophers, the only one until recently to place Newman in the top rank was H H Price, who in his Gifford Lectures *Belief* treats him as the one person worth studying on the topic since Locke and Hume; and Price himself was regarded by many of his colleagues as a reincarnation of old-fashioned empiricism. Newman disliked metaphysics of the German kind:

Let it be considered how rare and immaterial . . . is metaphysical proof: how difficult to embrace, even when presented to us by philosophers in whose clearness of mind and good sense we clearly confide; and what a vain system of words without ideas such men seem to be piling up, while perhaps we are obliged to confess that it must be we who are dull, not they who are fanciful; and that, whatever be the character of their investigations, we want the vigour or flexibility of mind to judge of them.[3]

The words of the young Newman are politer than those of the young A J Ayer a century later: but the attitude to metaphysics is not dissimilar.

Within so short a compass it is not possible to describe Newman's general contribution to philosophy, or to do justice to his discussion of such topics as real and notional assent, informal inference, illative sense, and the various kinds of certainty. Instead, I will discuss only Newman's contribution to philosophy of religion, and within that, I will concentrate on what he has to say of the nature of faith or religious belief. Newman's classic contribution to philosophy in general is the *Essay in Aid of a Grammar of Assent* which I have already quoted. But in the consideration of the nature and justification of faith some of Newman's very best work occurs in his University Sermons, whose full title is *Sermons chiefly on the theory of religious belief, preached before the University of Oxford.* The sermons were preached between 1826 and 1843, between Newman's appointment as Tutor at Oriel and his resignation of the living of St Mary's, all of them while he was a Fellow of Oriel. There is no great difference in actual doctrine that I can detect between Newman's Anglican and Catholic writings on this topic, and where there are differences they seem not to depend on religious or doctrinal grounds. There are at least as great differences between his earlier and later Oriel sermons as between the late Oriel sermons and the *Grammar.*

In the theological tradition in which Newman wrote faith was contrasted on the one hand with reason and knowledge and on the other with hope and charity. 'Faith' was used in a narrower sense than 'belief'. Aristotle believed, perhaps with good reason, that there was a divine Prime Mover unmoved; but his belief was not faith in God. On the other hand, Marlowe's Faustus, on the verge of damnation, speaks of Christ's blood streaming in the firmament; he has lost hope and charity, yet retains faith. So faith contrasts both with reason and with love. The special nature of the belief that is faith is that it is a belief in something as revealed by God; belief in a proposition on the word of God.

This is a Catholic, not a Protestant view of the nature of faith. Newman held it already in his University Sermons.

> The Word of Life is offered to a man; and on its being offered, he has Faith in it. Why? On these two grounds, – the word of its human messenger, and the likelihood of the message. And why does he feel the message to be probable? Because he has a love for it, his love being strong, though the testimony is weak. He has a keen sense of the intrinsic excellence of the message, of its desirableness, of its likeness to what it seems to him Divine goodness would vouchsafe did He vouchsafe any.[4]

Newman attacks the idea that reason judges both evidence for and the content of revelation, and that faith is just a state of heart, a moral quality, of adoration and obedience. Faith is itself an intellectual quality, even though reason is not an indispensable preliminary to faith.[5]

What is the role of reason? We have direct knowledge of material things through the senses: we are sensible of the existence of persons and things; we are directly cognizant of them through the senses. (To think that we have faculties for direct knowledge of immaterial things is a form of enthusiasm; certainly we are not conscious of any such faculties.) The senses are the only instruments which we know to be granted to us for direct and immediate acquaintance with things external to us. Even our senses convey us but a little way out of ourselves: we have to be near things to touch them: we can neither see hear nor touch things past or future.[6]

> Now reason is that faculty of the mind by which this deficiency is supplied; by which knowledge of things external to us, of beings, facts, and events, is attained beyond the range of sense. It ascertains for us not natural things only, or immaterial only, or present only, or past or future; but, even if limited in its power, it is unlimited in its range . . . It reaches to the ends of the universe, and to the throne of God beyond them; it brings us knowledge, whether clear or uncertain, still knowledge, in whatever degree of

perfection, from every side; but, at the same time, with this characteristic that it obtains it indirectly, not directly.[7]

Reason does not really perceive any thing; but is a faculty of proceeding from things that are perceived to things which are not. It is the faculty of gaining knowledge upon grounds given; and its exercise lies in asserting one thing, because of some other thing. When its exercise is conducted rightly, it leads to knowledge; when wrongly, to apparent knowledge, to opinion, and error.

If this be reason, then faith, simply considered, is itself an exercise of reason, whether right or wrong. For example 'I assent to this doctrine as true, because I have been taught it'; or 'because persons whom I trust say it was once guaranteed by miracles'. It 'must be allowed on all hands', says Newman, 'either that [faith] is illogical, or that the mind has some grounds which are not fully brought out when the process is thus exhibited.' The world says faith is weak, Scripture says it is unearthly.[8] Faith is an act of reason, but of what the world would call weak, bad, or insufficient reason, and that because it rests on presumption more and on evidence less.

Newman says it is true that nothing is true or right but what may be justified and in a certain sense proved by reason. But that does not mean that faith is grounded on reason; unless a judge can be called the origin as well as the justifier of the innocence of those who are brought before him.[9] On a popular view, reason requires strong evidence before assent, faith is content with weaker evidence. So Hume, Bentham and all those who like them think that faith is credulity. But in fact credulity is the counterfeit of faith, as scepticism is of reason.[10]

> Faith . . . does not demand evidence so strong as is necessary for . . . belief on the ground of Reason; and why? For this reason, because it is mainly swayed by antecedent considerations . . . previous notices, prepossessions, and (in a good sense of the word) prejudices. The mind that believes is acted upon by its own hopes, fears, and existing opinions . . . previously entertained principles, views, and wishes.[11]

Unbelievers say that a man is as little responsible for his faith as for his bodily functions; both are from nature, and the will cannot make a weak proof a strong one.

Newman: A Man for Our Time

> But love of the great Object of Faith, watchful attention to Him, readiness to believe Him near, easiness to believe Him interposing in human affairs, fear of the risk of slighting or missing what may really have come from Him; these are feelings not natural to fallen man, and they come only of supernatural grace; and these are the feelings which make us think evidence sufficient, which falls short of a proof in itself.[12]

> Thus we can see how Faith is and is not according to Reason: taken together with the antecedent probability that Providence will reveal himself, otherwise deficient evidence may be enough for conviction, even in the judgement of Reason. That is, Reason, weighing evidence only, or arguing from eternal experience, is counter to Faith; but, admitting the full influence of the moral feeling, it concurs with it.[13]

De facto this was how it all happened in the preaching of Christ and the apostles. It is wrong to think oneself a judge of religious truth without preparation of heart.

> Gross eyes see not: heavy ears hear not. But in the schools of the world the ways towards Truth are considered high roads open to all men, however disposed, at all times. Truth is to be approached without homage. Every one is considered on a level with his neighbour: or rather, the powers of the intellect, acuteness, sagacity, subtlety and depth, are thought the guides into Truth. Men consider that they have as full a right to discuss religious subjects, as if they were themselves religious. They will enter upon the most sacred points of Faith at the moment, at their pleasure, – if it so happen, in a careless frame of mind, in their hours of recreation, over the wine cup. Is it wonderful that they so frequently end in becoming indifferentists?[14]

The mismatch between evidence and commitment, and the importance of previous attitudes is to be observed not only in religious faith, but in other cases of belief.

> We hear a report in the streets, or read it in the public journals. We know nothing of the evidence; we do not know the witnesses, or anything about them: yet sometimes we believe implicitly, sometimes not: sometimes we believe without asking for evidence, sometimes we disbelieve till we receive it. Did a rumour circulate

of a destructive earthquake in Syria or the South of Europe, we should readily credit it; both because it might easily be true, and because it was nothing to us though it were. Did the report relate to countries nearer home, we should try to trace and authenticate it. We do not call for evidence till antecedent probabilities fail.[15]

Newman goes on to develop the theme that faith is not the only exercise of reason which, when critically examined, would be called unreasonable and yet is not so. Choice of sides in political questions, decisions for or against economic policies, tastes in literature: in all such cases if we measure people's grounds merely by the reasons they produce we have no difficulty in holding them up to ridicule, or even censure. So too with prophecies of weather, judgements of character, and even theories of the physical world.[16]

However systematically we argue on any topic, there must ever be something assumed ultimately which is incapable of proof, and without which our conclusion will be as illogical as faith is apt to seem to men of the world. We trust our senses without proof; we rely implicitly on our memory, and that too in spite of its being obviously unstable and treacherous. We trust to memory for the truth of most of our opinions; the grounds on which we hold them not being at a given moment all present to our minds: 'It may be said that without such assumption the world could not go on: true, and in the same way the Church could not go on without Faith. Acquiescence in testimony, or in evidence not stronger than testimony, is the only method, so far as we see, by which the next world can be revealed to us.'[17]

Moreover, the more precious a piece of knowledge is, the more subtle the evidence on which it is received.

> We are so constituted that if we insist upon being as sure as is conceivable, in every step of our course, we must be content to creep along the ground, and can never soar. If we are intended for great ends, we are called to great hazards; and whereas we are given absolute certainty in nothing, we must in all things choose between doubt and inactivity.[18]

In the pursuit of power, distinction in experimental science, or character for greatness we cannot avoid risk. Great objects exact a venture and sacrifice is the condition of honour; so even though the feelings which prompt us to see God in all things, and to recognize supernatural works in matters of the world, mislead us at times, though they make us trust in evidence which we ought not to admit, and partially incur with justice the imputation of credulity, yet a Faith which generously apprehends Eternal truth, though at times it degenerates into superstition, is far better than that cold, sceptical, critical tone of mind, which has no inward sense of an overruling, everpresent Providence, no desire to approach its God, but sits at home waiting for the fearful clearness of his visible coming, whom it might seek and find in due measure amid the twilight of the present world.[19]

The mind ranges to and fro, and spreads out, and advances forward with a quickness which has become a proverb and a subtlety and versatility which baffle investigation. It passes on from point to point, gaining one by some indication, another on a probability; then availing itself of an association; then falling back on some received law; next seizing on testimony; then committing itself to some popular impression, or some inward instinct, or some obscure memory; and thus it makes progress not unlike a clamberer on a steep cliff, who, by quick eye, prompt hand, and firm foot, ascends how he knows not himself, by personal endowments and by practice, rather than by rule, leaving no track behind him, and unable to teach another. It is not too much to say that the stepping by which great geniuses scale the mountains of truth is as unsafe and precarious to men in general as the ascent of a skilful mountaineer up a literal crag. It is a way which they alone can take; and its justification lies in their success.[20]

But how can one tell what is success in religious matters? On Newman's own account, there is a close similarity between faith and bigotry. In each case the grounds are conjectural, the issue is absolute acceptance of a certain message or doctrine as divine. Faith 'starts from probability, yet it ends in peremptory statements, if so be, mysterious, or at least beyond experience. It believes an informant amid doubt, yet accepts his information without doubt.'[21]

The University Sermons do not really succeed in solving the problem, to which Newman returned in the *Grammar of Assent*. How is it that a proposition which is not, and cannot be, demonstrated, which at the highest can only be proved to be truth-like, not true, nevertheless claims and receives our unqualified adhesion?

Some philosophers, for example Locke, say that there can be no demonstrable truth in concrete matters, and therefore assent to a concrete proposition must be conditional. Probable reasoning can never lead to certitude. According to Locke, there are degrees of assent, and absolute assent has no legitimate exercise except as ratifying acts of intuition or demonstration.

Locke gives as the unerring mark of the love of truth: the not entertaining any proposition with greater assurance than the proofs it is built on will warrant. 'Whoever goes beyond this measure of assent, it is plain receives not truth in the love of it, loves not truth for truth-sake, but for some other by-end.'[22]

This doctrine of Locke's is one of Newman's main targets of attack. In *The Development of Doctrine* he says that the by-end may be the love of God.[23] In the *Grammar of Assent* he claims that Locke's thesis is insufficiently empirical, too idealistic. Locke calls men 'irrational and indefensible if (so to speak) they take to the water, instead of remaining under the narrow wings of his own arbitrary theory'.[24]

On Locke's view, says Newman, assent would simply be a mere reduplication or echo of inference, assent just another name for inference. But in fact the two do not always go together; one may be strong and the other weak. We often assent, when we have forgotten the reasons for our assent. Reasons may still seem strong, and yet we do not any longer assent. Sometimes assent is never given in spite of strong and convincing arguments, perhaps through prejudice, perhaps through tardiness. Arguments may be better or worse, but assent either exists or not.

Even in mathematics there is a difference between inference and assent. A mathematician would not assent to his own conclusions, on new and difficult ground, and in the case of abstruse calculations, however often he went over his work, till he had the corroboration of other judgements besides his own.[25]

In demonstrative matters assent excludes doubt. In concrete cases, we do not give doubtful assent, nor are there instances where we assent a little and not much.

Usually we do not assent at all. Every day, as it comes, brings with it opportunities for us to enlarge our circle of assents. We read the newspapers; we look through debates in Parliament, pleadings in the law courts, leading articles, letters of correspondents, reviews of books, criticism in the fine arts, and we either form no opinion at all upon the subjects discussed, as lying out of our line, or at most we have only an opinion about them . . . we never say that we give [a proposition] a degree of assent. We might as well talk of degrees of truth as degrees of assent.[26]

But there are unconditional assents on evidence short of intuition and demonstration. We all believe without any doubt that we exist; that we have an individuality and identity all our own; that we think, feel, and act, in the home of our own minds.

Nor is the assent which we give to facts limited to the range of self-consciousness. We are sure beyond all hazard of a mistake, that our own self is not the only being existing; that there is an external world; that it is a system with parts and a whole, a universe carried on by laws; and that the future is affected by the past. We accept and hold with an unqualified assent, that the earth, considered as a phenomenon, is a globe; that all its regions see the sun by turns; that there are vast tracts on it of land and water; that there are really existing cities on definite sites, which go by the names of London, Paris, Florence and Madrid. We are sure that Paris or London, unless suddenly swallowed up by an earthquake or burned to the ground, is today just what it was yesterday, when we left it.[27]

Newman's favourite example of a firm belief on flimsy evidence is our conviction that Great Britain is an island.

Our reasons for believing that we are circumnavigable are such as these: first, we have been so taught in our childhood, and it is so in all the maps; next, we never heard it contradicted or questioned; on the contrary, every one whom we have heard speak on the subject of Great Britain, every book we have read, invariably took it for granted; our whole national history, the routine transactions and current events of the country, our social and commercial system, our political relations with foreigners, imply it in one way or another. Numberless facts, or what we consider facts, rest on the truth of it; no received fact rests on its being otherwise . . .

However, negative arguments and circumstantial evidence are

not all, in such a matter, which we have a right to require. They are not the highest kind of proof possible. Those who have circumnavigated the island have a right to be certain: have we ever ourselves fallen in with anyone who has? . . . Have we personally more than an impression, if we view the matter argumentatively, a lifelong impression about Great Britain, like the belief, so long and so widely entertained, that the earth was immovable, and the sun careered round it? I am not at all insinuating that we are not rational in our certitude; I only mean that we cannot analyse a proof satisfactorily, the result of which good sense actually guarantees to us.[28]

Take another example.

What are my grounds for thinking that I, in my own particular case, shall die? I am as certain of it in my own innermost mind, as I am that I now live; but what is the distinct evidence on which I allow myself to be certain? How would it tell in a court of justice? . . . Men tell me that there is a law of death, meaning by a law a necessity; and I answer that they are throwing dust into my eyes, giving me words instead of things. What is a law but a generalized fact? And what power has the past over the future? and what power has the case of others over my own case? and how many deaths have I seen? How many ocular witnesses have imparted to me their experience of deaths, sufficient to establish what is called a law? . . .

The strongest proof I have for my inevitable mortality is the *reductio ad absurdum.* Can I point to the man, in historic times, who has lived his two hundred years? What has become of past generations of men, unless it is true that they suffered dissolution? But this is a circuitous argument to warrant a conclusion to which in matter of fact I adhere so relentlessly.[29]

We laugh to scorn the idea that we had no parents though we have no memory of our birth; that we shall never depart this life, though we can have no experience of the future; that we are able to live without food, though we have never tried; that a world of men did not live before our time, or that that world has no history: there has been no rise and fall of states, no great men, no wars, no revolutions, no art, no science, no literature, no religion.[30]

On all these truths, Newman sums up, we have an immediate and unhesitating hold, 'nor do we think ourselves guilty of not loving truth for truth's sake, because we cannot reach them through a series of intuitive propositions . . . None of us can think or act without the acceptance of truths, not intuitive, not demonstrated, yet sovereign.'[31]

Philosophers like Locke do not really have misgivings about the truths they call in question:

> They think it a duty to remind us that since the full etiquette of logical requirements has not been satisfied, we must believe those truths at our peril . . . They do not, for instance, intend for a moment to imply that there is even the shadow of a doubt that Great Britain is an island, but they think we ought to know, if we do not know, that there is no proof of the fact, in mode and figure, equal to the proof of a proposition of Euclid; and that in consequence they and we are all bound to suspend our judgement about such a fact, though it be in an infinitesimal degree, lest we should seem not to love truth for truth's sake. Having made their protest, they subside without scruple into that same absolute assurance of only partially proved truths, which is natural to the illogical imagination of the multitude.[32]

Newman makes a distinction between simple assent and complex assent. Simple assent is often unconscious. There are innumerable acts of assent which we make without reflection. But complex, or reflex, assent is what is meant by certitude: and it is certitude that is the characteristic manifestation of religious faith. Newman describes certitude in the following way:

> It seems then that on the whole there are three conditions of certitude: that it follows on investigation and proof, that it is accompanied by a specific sense of intellectual satisfaction and repose, and that it is irreversible. If the assent is made without rational grounds, it is a rash judgement, a fancy, or a prejudice; if without the sense of finality, it is scarcely more than an inference; if without permanence, it is a mere conviction.[33]

But how can faith be certitude, if certitude follows on investigation? Does not investigation imply doubt, which conflicts with faith? To set about concluding a proposition is not *ipso facto* to doubt its truth: we may aim at inferring a proposition, while all the time we assent to it; we do not deny our faith because we become controversialists. Investigation is not inquiry; inquiry is indeed inconsistent with assent. It is sometimes complained of that a Catholic cannot inquire into the truth of his creed: of course he cannot if he would retain the name of believer.[34]

But may not investigation lead to giving up assent? Yes, it may; but

> my vague consciousness of the possibility of a reversal of my belief in the course of my researches, as little interferes with the honesty and firmness of that belief while those researches proceed, as the recognition of the possibility of my train's oversetting is an evidence of an intention on my part of undergoing so great a calamity.[35]

Newman describes the specific feeling of certainty: a feeling of satisfaction and self-gratulation. The repose in self and in its object, as connected with self, which is characteristic of certitude, does not attach to mere knowing, that is, to the perception of things, but to the consciousness of having that knowledge.[36]

Assents may and do change; certitudes endure. This is why religion demands more than an assent to its truth; it requires a certitude, or at least an assent which is convertible into certitude on demand. Belief does not necessarily imply a positive resolution in the party believing never to abandon the belief. It implies not an intention never to change, but the utter absence of all thought, or expectation or fear of change.

Newman from time to time talks as if there is such a thing as false certitude, a state which differs from knowledge only in its truth value. But, he says, not altogether consistently, if the proposition is objectively true, 'then the assent may be called a perception, the conviction a certitude, the proposition or truth a certainty, or thing known, or a matter of knowledge, and to assent to it is to know'.[37]

Whether or not certitude entails truth, it is undeniable that to be certain of something involves believing in its truth. It follows that if I am certain of a thing, I believe it will remain what I now hold it to be, even though my mind should have the bad fortune to let it drop. If we are certain, we spontaneously reject objections to our belief as idle; though the contradictory of a truth be brought back to mind by the pertinacity of an opponent, or a voluntary or involuntary act of imagination, still that contradictory proposition and its arguments are mere phantoms and dreams. This is like the way the mind revolts from the supposition that a straight line is the longest distance between two points, or that Great Britain is in shape an exact square, or that I shall escape dying.[38]

Some may say, we should never have this contempt-bringing conviction of anything; but if in fact 'a man has such a conviction, if he is sure that Ireland is to the West of England, or that the Pope is the Vicar of Christ, nothing is left to him, if he would be consistent, but to carry his conviction out into this magisterial intolerance of any contrary assertion'. Newman goes on to say: whoever loses his conviction on a given point is thereby proved not to have been certain of it.[39]

But is there any specific state or habit of thought, of which the distinguishing mark is unchangeableness? On the contrary, any conviction, false as well as true, may last; and any conviction, true as well as false, may be lost. No line can be drawn between such real certitudes as have truth for their object, and apparent certitudes. There is no test of genuine certitude of truth. What looks like certitude always is exposed to the chance of turning out to be a mistake. Certitude does not admit of an interior, immediate test, sufficient to discriminate it from false certitude.[40]

Newman correctly distinguishes certainty from infallibility. My memory is not infallible; I remember for certain what I did yesterday, but that does not mean that my memory is infallible. I am quite clear that two and two make four, but I often make mistakes in long addition sums. Certitude concerns a particular proposition, infallibility is a faculty or gift. It is possible to be certain that Victoria is Queen, without claiming infallibility, as it is possible to do a virtuous action without being impeccable.[41]

But how can the secure repose of certitude be mine if I know, as I know too well, that before now I have thought myself certain when I was certain after all of an untruth? What happened once may happen again. Newman's answer is this: mistakes should make us more cautious, but even so, grounds for caution may be overcome.

Suppose I am walking out in the moonlight, and see dimly the outlines of some figure among the trees; – it is a man. I draw nearer, it is still a man; nearer still, and all hesitation is at an end, – I am certain it is a man. But he neither moves nor speaks when

I address him; and then I ask myself what can be his purpose in hiding among the trees at such an hour. I come quite close to him and put out my arm. Then I find for certain that what I took for a man is but a singular shadow, formed by the falling of the moonlight on the interstices of some branches or their foliage. Am I not to indulge my second certitude, because I was wrong in my first? Does not any objection, which lies against my second from the failure of my first, fade away before the evidence on which my second is founded?[42]

We do not dispense with clocks, because from time to time they go wrong and tell untruly.

The sense of certitude may be called the bell of the intellect; and that it strikes when it should not is a proof that the clock is out of order, no proof that the bell will be untrustworthy and useless when it comes to us adjusted and regulated from the hands of the clockmaker.[43]

Certitude is a mental state; certainty is a quality of propositions. Those propositions I call certain, which are such that I am certain of them. Certitude is . . . an active recognition of propositions as true, such as it is the duty of each individual himself to exercise at the bidding of reason, and, when reason forbids, to withhold. And reason never bids us be certain except on an absolute proof; and such a proof can never be furnished to us by the logic of words, for as certitude is of the mind, so is the act of inference which leads to it.

Is there any criterion of the accuracy of an inference? 'The sole and final judgement on the validity of an inference in concrete matter is committed to the personal action of the ratiocinative faculty, the perfection or virtue of which I have called the Illative Sense, a use of the word "sense", parallel to our use of it in "good sense" "common sense" . . .'[44]

We have to accept being the kind of things we are: beings which have to progress by inference and assent. The course of inference is ever more or less obscure, while assent is ever distinct and definite, yet one follows on the other: we have to accept this. But the illative sense is in theoretical reasoning what Aristotle's *phronesis* is in practical reasoning. Aristotle says that no code of laws, or moral treatise, maps out the path of individual virtue. So too with the controlling principle in inferences. There are as many forms of *phronesis* as there are virtues. There is no one formula which is a working rule for poetry, medicine, politics; so too with ratiocination. In reasoning on any subject whatever, which is concrete, we proceed, as far indeed as we can, by the logic of language; but we are obliged to supplement it by the more subtle and elastic logic of thought.

How does Newman apply this to the evidences for religion? Christianity is a revelation, a

> definite message from God to man dictinctly conveyed by His chosen instruments, and to be received as such a message; and therefore to be positively acknowledged, embraced, and maintained as true, on the grounds of its being divine, not as true on intrinsic grounds, not as probably true, or partially true, but as absolutely certain knowledge, certain in a sense in which nothing else can be certain, because it comes from Him who neither can deceive nor be deceived.[45]

With regard to the justification of religious belief, Newman gives up the intention of demonstrating either natural religion or Christianity.

> Not that I deny that demonstration is possible. Truth, certainly, as such, rests upon grounds intrinsically and objectively and abstractedly demonstrative, but it does not follow from this that the arguments producible in its favour are unanswerable and irresistible . . . The fact of revelation is in itself demonstrably true, but it is not therefore true irresistibly; else how comes it to be resisted?[46]

'For me', says Newman, 'it is more congenial to my own judgement to attempt to prove Christianity in the same informal way in which I can prove for certain that I have been born into this world, and that I shall die out of it.'[47]

Newman's proof of Christianity will only work for those who are prepared for it, imbued with religious opinions and sentiments identified with natural religion. He assumes the falsehood of the opinions which 'characterise a civilized age'. The evidences 'presuppose a belief and perception of the Divine Presence'. Newman does not stress miracles, but rather 'those coincidences and their cumulations which, though not in themselves miraculous, do irresistibly force upon us, almost by the law of our nature, the presence of the extraordinary agency of Him whose being we already acknowledge'.[48]

As examples Newman quotes the sudden death of a market woman following the utterance of a curse, and the fact of Napoleon's being defeated in Russia within two years of his being excommunicated by the Pope. These coincidences are indications, to the illative sense of those who believe in a Moral Governor, of his immediate presence. But the greatest of these impressive coincidences is the whole history of Judaism and Christianity.

If the history of Judaism is so wonderful as to suggest the presence of some special divine agency in its appointments and fortunes, still more wonderful and divine is the history of Christianity; and again it is more wonderful still, that two such wonderful creations should span almost the whole course of ages, during which nations and states have been in existence, and should constitute a professed system of continued intercourse between earth and heaven from first to last amid all the vicissitudes of human affairs. This phenomenon again carries on its face, to those who believe in a God, the probability that it has that divine origin which it professes to have.[49]

Newman concludes:

Christianity is addressed, both as regards its evidences and its contents, to minds which are in the normal condition of human nature, as believing in God and in a future judgement. Such minds it addresses both through the intellect and through the imagination; creating a certitude of its truth by arguments too various for direct enumeration, too personal and deep for words, too powerful and concurrent for refutation. Nor need reason come first and faith second (though this is the logical order) but one and the same teaching is in different aspects both object and proof, and elicits one complex act both of inference and assent.[50]

Given Newman's own description of the scope of his argument, one may ask: Why should one believe in God and in a future judgement at all? In response to this question Newman makes his celebrated appeal to the testimony of conscience. He is not confident in the probative force of the traditional arguments to the existence of God from the nature of the physical world.

It is indeed a great question whether Atheism is not as philosophically consistent with the phenomena of the physical world, taken by themselves, as the doctrine of a creative and governing Power. But, however this be, the practical safeguard against Atheism in the case of scientific inquirers is the inward need and desire, the inward experience of that Power, existing in the mind before and independently of their examination of His material world.[51]

As from a multitude of instinctive perceptions, acting in particular instances, of something beyond the senses, we generalise the notion of an external world, and then picture that world in and according to those particular phenomena from which we started, so from the perceptive power which identifies the intimations of conscience with the reverberations or echoes (so to say) of an external admonition, we proceed on the notion of a Supreme Ruler and Judge.[52]

Conscience is a mental phenomenon as much as memory, reason, or the sense of the beautiful. It is a moral sense and a sense of duty; a judgement of the reason and a magisterial dictate: it has both a critical and judicial office. Conscience, considered as a moral sense, is an intellectual sentiment, but it is always emotional; therefore it involves recognition of a living object. Inanimate things cannot stir our affections, these are correlative with persons.

If, on doing wrong, we feel the same tearful, broken-hearted sorrow which overwhelms us on hurting a mother; if on doing right, we enjoy the same sunny serenity of mind, the same soothing, satisfactory delight which follows on our receiving praise from a father, we certainly have within us the image of some person, to whom our love and veneration look, in whose smile we find our happiness, for whom we yearn, towards whom we direct our pleadings, in whose anger we are troubled and waste away. These feelings in us are such as require for their exciting cause an intelligent being . . .[53]

So far I have expounded Newman, without criticizing him. In a centenary volume it is appropriate to celebrate Newman, not to bury him. But I must end by stating briefly my own position on the issues on which he wrote so eloquently.

Newman begins his own criticism of Locke with the following

words: 'I have so high a respect both for the character and the ability of Locke . . . that I feel no pleasure in considering him in the light of an opponent.'[54] Price in his book on belief says:

> Let us follow this excellent example; for no-one, and certainly no Oxford man, should criticise Newman without praising him . . . Newman is one of the masters of English prose. The power, and the charm, of his style are so compelling that the reader soon becomes their willing captive, and it seems ungrateful, almost ungracious, to question what has been so felicitously said.[55]

One's reluctance to take a stand against Newman is increased by the fact that Newman puts the objections to his own views so marvellously well: indeed, he is often at his best when stating a position against which he intends to argue. For instance, we may read the way in which he states the argument which is most likely to have occurred to those who have followed his defence of the justification of religious belief.

> Antecedent probabilities may be equally available for what is true and what pretends to be true, for a revelation and its counterfeit, for Paganism, or Mahometanism, or Christianity. They seem to supply no intelligible rule what is to be believed and what not; or how a man is to pass from a false belief to a true. If a claim of miracles is to be acknowledged because it happens to be advanced, why not for the miracles of India as well as for those of Palestine? If the abstract probability of a Revelation be the measure of genuineness in a given case, why not in the case of Mahomet as well as of the Apostles?[56]

None the less, I cannot conclude without stating that I think Newman is wrong on a number of major points. I will list, without defending, five criticisms which can be made of his position.

First, Assent does have degrees; even on religious matters; and this is something which Newman himself knows and admits when he is off his guard. There is a difference between an assent to a proposition without fear of its falsehood, but with a readiness to examine contrary evidence and change one's mind, and an assent like Newman's certitude which contemns all objections which may be brought against it. Newman himself gives examples of adherence to propositions which does not fulfil the conditions of certitude. Some of these concern matters of religious belief.

I may believe in the liquefaction of St Pantaleon's blood, and believe it to the best of my judgement to be a miracle, yet supposing a chemist offered to produce exactly the same phenomena under exactly similar circumstances by the materials put at his command by his science, so as to reduce what seemed beyond nature within natural laws, I should watch with some suspense of mind and misgiving the course of his experiment, as having no Divine Word to fall back upon as a ground of certainty that the liquefaction was miraculous.[57]

This is a very important passage, which gives away Newman's official position. It shows that there is such a thing as belief, and indeed religious belief, which falls short of unconditional assent. The real question which Newman ought to be facing is: why is not this the appropriate kind of certitude in religious matters, given the nature of the evidence for there being a divine revelation of Christianity?

Secondly, Newman is right to emphasize, and it is one of his major contributions to philosophy, that a belief such as the belief that Great Britain is an island is not a belief based on sufficient evidence. But the reason for this is that it is not based on evidence at all. For evidence has to be better known than that for which it is evidence; and none of the scraps of reasons I could produce for the proposition that Great Britain is an island are better known to me than the proposition itself.

But this means that there is not the parallel which Newman drew between the belief that Great Britain is an island and the religious faith of a Christian believer. For faith to be faith and not mere belief it has to be belief on the word of God. If that is so, then the fact of revelation has to be better known than the content of revelation. But this Newman does not even attempt to prove.

Thirdly, Newman is quite unconvincing in claiming that certitude is indefectible. It is true that knowledge is indefectible: if I claim to know that p, and then change my mind about p, I also withdraw the claim that I ever knew that p. But certainty is not like knowledge here: there is nothing odd in saying, 'I was certain but I was wrong'. The difference between the two is connected with the fact that knowledge is only of what is true. But Newman agrees (though not with complete regularity) that there can be false certitude. Hence his position is internally inconsistent here.

118

However, the internal inconsistency in this case may not be very important given Newman's apologetic purpose. There is no sufficient reason for him to insist that certitude must be indefectible. Once Newman has shown, convincingly, that past mistakes do not make subsequent certainty impossible to justify, it is not of great moment whether certainties may be lost, and it becomes just a matter of the definition of certitude as contrasted with conviction. Newman, to his credit, does not ever argue, 'I am certain, ergo this is true'.

Fourthly, Newman's argument from conscience is unconvincing. The parallel drawn in *The Grammar of Assent* with our knowledge of the external world is based on a false phenomenalist view which most philosophers would now regard as indefensible. It is interesting that this view conflicts with that presented in the *University Sermons*. In his later, but not his earlier, writing Newman assumes that our knowledge of material objects is indirect, a hypothesis from phenomena.

Fifthly, conscience itself may be seen as conditioned or absolute. If conditioned, it is the result of reasoning – as it is for the Utilitarian, operating his felicific calculus. Newman is aware of this, and denounces the idea: 'We reprobate under the name of Utilitarianism, the substitution of Reason for Conscience.'[58] But reasoning need not be Utilitarian, and Aristotle, whose *phronesis* Newman takes as the paradigm for illative sense, does present a theory of conscience which makes it the result of practical reasoning.

If, on the other hand, conscience is thought of not as a conclusion from reasoning, but as an absolute dictate, then the objection of J L Mackie tells:

> If we take conscience at its face value and accept as really valid what it asserts, we must say that there is a rational prescriptivity about certain kinds of action for doing them or for refraining from them. There is a to-be-done-ness or a not-to-be-done-ness involved in that kind of action in itself. If so, there is no need to look beyond this to any supernatural person who commands or forbids such action . . .[59]

If the existence of God is looked on not as something perceived behind conscience, but as something to explain the origin of conscience, then of course Newman's hypothesis needs to be considered in competition with other hypotheses. One such hypothesis is the theory of Freud, which to any modern reader is brought irresistibly to mind by the passage quoted above about the delight which is received from the praise of a father.

One of the earliest readers of the *Grammar of Assent* was Gerard Manley Hopkins. He wrote to a friend: 'It is perhaps heavy reading. The justice and candour and gravity and rightness of mind is what is so beautiful in all he writes but what dissatisfies me is a narrow circle of instance and quotation . . . But he remains, nevertheless, our greatest living master of style.'[60]

Hopkins offered to write a commentary to remedy the deficiencies of the book. Given the smooth sunlight brilliance of most of Newman's writing, and the dense tangled opacity of which Hopkins was master, it is not surprising that Newman rejected the suggestion with a degree of impatience. But it would have been wonderful to have had a work which combined the gifts of the two greatest masters of English of the period.

If some of Newman's philosophical writing makes heavy reading, he gives his own eloquent excuse:

> The primary duty of a literary man is to have clear conceptions, and to be exact and intelligible in expressing them. But in a philosopher it is a merit even to be not utterly vague, inchoate and obscure in his teaching, and if he fails even of this low standard of language we remind ourselves that his obscurity perhaps is owing to his depth. No power of words in a lecturer would be sufficient to make psychology easy to his hearers.[61]

This must serve both to excuse such opacity as remains with our present topic, and to whet the reader's appetite for the discussion which follows of 'Newman the Writer', itself from a literary man.

NOTES

1. *Tractatus* 4.442.
2. *An Essay in Aid of a Grammar of Assent*, ed. I T Ker (Oxford, Clarendon Press, 1985), p. 182.
3. *Sermons, chiefly on the theory of religious belief, preached before the University of Oxford* (London, Rivington, 2nd edn 1844), p. 210.
4. ibid., p. 195.
5. ibid., p. 173.
6. ibid., pp. 197–8.
7. ibid., p. 199.

8. ibid., pp. 200–1.
9. ibid., p. 174.
10. ibid., p. 177.
11. ibid., pp. 179–80.
12. ibid., p. 185.
13. ibid., p. 187.
14. ibid., pp. 190–1.
15. ibid., p. 180.
16. ibid., p. 202.
17. ibid., pp. 206–7.
18. ibid., p. 208.
19. ibid., p. 213.
20. ibid., pp. 252–3.
21. ibid., XIV, para. 34.
22. Locke, *Essay on Human Understanding* IV, xvi, p. 6.
23. *An Essay on the Development of Christian Doctrine*, ch. vii, p. 2.
24. *Grammar*, p. 109.
25. *Grammar*, pp. 110–12.
26. ibid., p. 115.
27. ibid., p. 117.
28. ibid., pp. 191–2.
29. ibid., p. 195.
30. ibid., p. 117.
31. ibid., p. 118.
32. ibid., p. 119.
33. ibid., p. 168.
34. ibid., p. 125.
35. ibid., p. 127.
36. ibid., p. 134.
37. ibid., p. 128.
38. ibid., p. 130.
39. ibid., pp. 130ff.
40. ibid., p. 145.
41. ibid., p. 147.
42. ibid., p. 151.
43. ibid., p. 152.
44. ibid., p. 223.
45. ibid., p. 250.
46. ibid., p. 264.
47. ibid., p. 264.
48. ibid., p. 275.
49. ibid., p. 283.
50. ibid., p. 316.
51. *University Sermons*, p. 186.
52. *Grammar*, p. 72.

53. ibid., p. 76.
54. ibid., p. 107.
55. H H Price, *Belief* (London, Allen & Unwin, 1969), p. 133.
56. *University Sermons*, p. 226.
57. *Grammar*, p. 132.
58. *University Sermons*, p. 175.
59. J L Mackie, *The Miracle of Theism* (Oxford, Clarendon Press, 1982), p. 104.
60. G M Hopkins, *Further Letters*, ed. C C Abbot (London 1956), p. 58.
61. *Grammar*, p. 21.

· 6 ·

Newman the Writer

A N WILSON

A N Wilson has already made a considerable reputation for himself with biographies of literary figures such as Scott, Milton, Belloc, Tolstoy and C S Lewis. In what follows it quickly becomes clear that he will brook no exaggerated claims for the merits of Newman as poet or novelist. Rather like Lord St John of Fawsley he finds the clue to his genius as a writer in his style. But in the final analysis, he argues, it is not just the form but what Newman succeeds in conveying by that form – the sense of what it is to be religious – which gives Newman his lasting place in English letters.

'Things and actions are what they are, and the consequences of them will be what they will be', as one of Newman's favourite philosophers (and perhaps, next to Newman himself, the greatest of Oriel men) remarked.[1] Armed with such common sense, we who love John Henry Newman have perhaps done no more than smile at the passage in Lytton Strachey's *Eminent Victorians* where the belle-lettrist historian speculates about what would have happened if Newman's father 'when the gig came round on the fatal morning, still undecided between the two Universities, had chanced to turn the horse's head in the direction of Cambridge'. In Strachey's eyes, Newman was

> a child of the Romantic Revival, a creature of emotion and memory, a dreamer whose secret spirit dwelt apart in delectable mountains, an artist whose subtle senses, caught, like a shower in the sunshine, the impalpable rainbow of the immaterial world ... He might, at Cambridge, whose cloisters have ever been consecrated to poetry and common sense, have followed quietly

123

in Gray's footsteps and brought into flower those seeds of inspiration which now lie embedded amid the faded devotion of the *Lyra Apostolica*. At Oxford, he was doomed. It was in vain that he plunged into the pages of Gibbon or communed for long hours with Beethoven over his beloved violin. The air was thick with clerical sanctity, heavy with the odours of tradition and the soft warmth of spiritual authority; his friendship with Hurrell Froude did the rest.[2]

We all recognize the real Newman in this purple passage, and yet there is much with which a defensive Oxonian might choose to take issue. Are all Cambridge poets – Gray, since Strachey mentions him, or Tennyson – noted for their common sense? Are they all, as Strachey would imply, secular – what of Herbert and Crashaw? Since when have Gibbon and Beethoven become honorary Cambridge men?

Much more germane to our purpose is to ask whether Strachey has got Newman right. Is he essentially a poet who has become sidetracked into theology? Is the Romantic dreamer, who comes before us as a child in the *Apologia*, a man who might have become a poet or novelist if it had not been for the misfortunes of his educational history? 'I used to wish the Arabian tales were true', Newman tells us. (When he came to be a man, adds Strachey, commenting on Newman's belief in the miraculous flight of the Holy House of Nazareth to Loretto, 'his wish seems to have been granted'.[3]) '. . . My imagination ran on unknown influences, on magical powers, and talismans . . . I thought life might be a dream, and I an angel, and all this world a deception, my fellow-angels by a playful device, concealing themselves from me, and deceiving me with the semblance of a material world.'[4]

This, and other passages like it in the *Apologia*, is the strand of Newman's personal myth which most keenly appealed to Strachey. And even those of a less secular temper than Strachey must have felt a certain weariness as they turned the pages of Newman's voluminous published works in search of some matter other than Church or religion which engaged his imagination for more than a few pages: some paragraph in his two novels which betrayed the smallest particle of interest in human psychology, some letters, for example to his mother and sisters, in which might be found a sustained and unegoistic interest in their doings and affairs, without a repeated return to his King Charles' head obsessions with church politics. When we consider how through and through, how monomaniacally churchy Newman was, I think we need rather more than Oxford or the friendship of Hurrell Froude to explain it. Speculations about what sort of books he might have written had he gone to Cambridge do not cut much ice as we take down volume after volume from the shelf and see what he actually did write. The notion of his being a minor poet quietly following in Gray's footsteps loses its plausibility. We could as well imagine that if only P G Wodehouse had formed a café friendship with Ezra Pound he might have abandoned his early stories of school life and embarked on a career as a serious author of *vers libre*; had Karl Marx lived but a little later in the century, and happened to bump into Arthur Sullivan on the steps of the British Museum, what comic operettas we might have seen.

The truth is, Newman did not need to be pushed into his religious preoccupations by the fellows of Oriel. These preoccupations had possessed him ever since he was a schoolboy in Ealing, and would, I am sure, have continued to do so wherever he had pursued his education. Given his extraordinary personal magnetism, they would doubtless have changed Cambridge as they changed Oxford, if the gig had by some curious fate taken him there. Were it our purpose to psychoanalyse Newman, which it is not, we would wish to know less about his father's gig on that fateful morning, and more about his father, whose inadequacies have never been sufficiently explored by the biographers. There was Mr Newman's failure in his business ventures, the end (more than slightly shaming, one would guess, to John Henry) as a publican in Clerkenwell, living apart, it would seem, from his wife. Newman always displayed the classic Anglo-Catholic ambivalence towards father-figures in all his dealings with bishops, both in his Anglican and his Catholic incarnations. He governed his whole grown-up life around the belief that bishops were possessed of supreme apostolic authority, while going out of his way to say and write things which they would find unacceptable; and this was as true of the author of Tract Ninety as it was of the man who baited Archbishop Cullen of Dublin or fell foul of Manning.

Francis Newman, the younger brother of our hero, has a revealing memory in his book *Phases of Faith* when he says that in the earliest period of my Oxford residence I fell into uneasy collision with him [John Henry] concerning Episcopal powers. I had on one occasion dropt something disrespectful about bishops or a bishop – something which if it had been said about a clergyman would have passed unnoticed; but my brother checked and reproved me – as I thought very uninstructively – for 'wanting reverence towards bishops'. I knew not then, and I know not now, why Bishops, *as such*, should be more reverenced than common clergymen or clergymen as such more than common men . . . To find my brother thus stop my mouth was a puzzle, and impeded all free speech towards him; in fact, I very soon left off the attempt at religious intercourse with him, of asking counsel as of one who could sympathise . . .[5]

This anecdote draws attention more vividly than Strachey's wistful speculations to a notorious feature of Newman's character, and one which has a direct bearing upon the kind of writer he set out to be: namely, his prickliness, his readiness to take offence, his swiftness to assert disagreement or to retreat into a wounded silence if confronted with any point of view other than the one which he happened at that moment to be entertaining himself. This, of course, is not a characteristic of a religious solitary, or of the dreamer whose secret spirit dwells apart in the delectable mountains. Hermits and anchorites can fall into as many angry little moods as they choose and it will not effect the rest of us. Newman's petulance, like his sweetness and goodness and like his piety itself, were all part of his attractiveness, both to the huge audiences he was able to command when speaking in public and to the little coterie of admirers without whom he was never able, emotionally, to function. His intimate life of prayer, and his love affair with God were not private. Anyone coming into Oriel of an evening could look up at the windows of his private oratory, one of the largest of the oriel windows in the quad, and see his tall slender form kneeling in the candle-light, in full and inescapable view. The withdrawal to Littlemore was not done quietly. He went with the full accolade of his condemnation by Convocation, and when, on 25 September 1843 he preached his famous Parting of Friends sermon in Littlemore parish church, he pulled out all the stops, even buying new bonnets for the village children for the occasion. The grief which he felt on leaving the Church of England, and even more on leaving Oxford, can scarcely be exaggerated. But nobody can read his novel *Loss and Gain* without being aware that its author did not find it wholly dissatisfying to be the centre of so much attention. In latter years, he was to write his autobiography with tears streaming down his cheeks. In the palmy days of 1847, Newman was discovered in his rooms in Rome laughing over the manuscript upon which he was engaged:

> 'Catholic, Catholic, I don't know what you mean', said Freeborn. 'I mean', said White, 'the baptism of the One Catholic Church, of which the Creed speaks; it's quite intelligible.' 'But what do you mean by the Catholic Church?', asked Freeborn. 'The Anglican', answered Bateman. 'The Roman', answered White, both in the same breath. There was a general laugh . . .[6]

Loss and Gain bristles with such hilarities. Like most bad novels, it is a self-projection. Charles Reding is just such a dreamy, introspective youth as the adolescent hero of the *Apologia*, 'not without a tinge of melancholy in his character, which sometimes degenerated into mawkishness'. He ends his story, after the familiar Tractarian intellectual and spiritual journey, by being received into the Catholic Church, as Newman was, by a Passionist priest, as Newman was, and feeling about the experience exactly as Newman felt. For the author of the *Apologia* it was 'like coming into port after a rough sea; and my happiness on that score remains to this day without interruption'.[7] Charles Reding's conversion in the novel was 'like the stillness which almost sensibly affects the ears when a bell which had been long tolling stops, or when a vessel, after much tossing at sea, finds itself in harbour'.[8]

Of course, Charles Reding is not the only self-projection in the book. There is the question lurking in every Oxford mind of whether the eminent divine Smith – i.e. Newman himself – will join the Roman Church, and the whole world depicted in the book, of risibly earnest young people obsessed by questions of church theology, is very largely the world actually created in the 1830s by Newman himself, the heady atmosphere described by Matthew Arnold in that famous description of Newman preaching in the dim afternoon light of St Mary's.

If we were here to assess Newman's character, which we are not, an embarrassment might steal over us as we overhear him laughing at the composition of *Loss and Gain*. It is not merely that jokes of the 1847 vintage are so leadenly unfunny, as unfunny as old copies of *Punch* – or, come to that, as new copies of *Punch*. The overweening self-regard of the book is what makes the reader squirm. Judged as a work of fiction, *Loss and Gain* is what we should expect from the man who did not like Jane Austen because the parsons in her books were insufficiently serious. (Did she, incidentally, in Alton, Hampshire, ever set eyes on the infant Newman when he lived there? It is tempting to suppose that she did.) If my brief were to discuss Newman's skills as a novelist I would have to borrow the strong language of Dr Leavis in his dismissal of C P Snow – 'as a novelist he doesn't exist. He doesn't begin to exist.'

But this is to be carried away by Strachey's idea of Newman as the man who would have been a certain type of writer, we might even say a 'proper writer' if only he had not been to Oxford and imbibed the air 'thick with clerical sanctity'. The same would happen if we were to analyse his other, much more charming novel, *Callista*, or if we were to compare the bulk of his poetry with even the most minor secular practitioners of his age. There are good passages in *The Dream of Gerontius*, it is true, particularly when they are sung to the sublime music of Elgar; and anyone who is not turned to gooseflesh by 'Lead Kindly Light' is a baboon. But if we read his complete verse, it is hard to esteem Newman very highly. He seems less good than R W Dixon. Certainly less good than Hawker of Morwenstowe. Newman the novelist and Newman the poet – with the exception of his great hymns – played as important a role in our cultural history as Winston Churchill the painter or Dennis Healey the concert pianist. If we are to discover Newman's excellence as a writer we must cease to walk in Gray's footsteps and look elsewhere down the library shelf for the works which reveal our man, in his greatness, his unforgettably distinctive greatness.

One must start with the sermons. It was not merely Matthew Arnold's dewy-eyed nostalgia for the Oxford of his youth which made him recall Newman's afternoon sermons at St Mary's. It was also Arnold's astuteness as a critic. And perhaps to get their full flavour, the reader of Newman's *Parochial and Plain Sermons* needs from time to time to recall the scene, the crowded University Church, the air full of emotion, the words from the pulpit delivered in that beautifully modulated voice, spoken rapidly with long pauses between each sentence. But it is not merely as a theatrical scene that the sermons survive, even though what inspired Newman to write them was his consciousness of power over young minds. The sermons are more than this. Their rhetorical power and vigour remains unabated. Arnold speaks of their music as 'subtle, sweet, mournful', which sounds a little like Strachey's Cambridge dreamer. If you had not read Newman's sermons, you might suppose from Arnold's description that they would be purple passages strung together, perhaps with learned reflections on subjects of his own academic interest, such as the *Arians of the Fourth Century*. He was not that sort of preacher at all. Newman preaches like a man who has heard the voice of God. His sermons are not water-colours. It is impossible to convey their flavour without quotation, and it is difficult to make a brief excerpt. But consider this meditation on the crucifixion:

> Let us suppose that some aged and venerable person whom we have known as long as we can recollect anything, and loved and reverenced, suppose such a one, who had often done us kindnesses, who had taught us, who had given us good advice, who had encouraged us, smiled on us, comforted us in trouble, whom we knew to be very good and religious, very holy, full of wisdom, full of heaven, with grey hairs and awful countenance, waiting for Almighty God's summons to leave this world for a better place; suppose, I say such a one whom we have ourselves known, and whose memory is dear to us, rudely seized by fierce men, stripped naked in public, insulted, driven about here and there, made a laughing-stock, struck, spit on, dressed up in other clothes in ridicule, then severely scourged on the back, then laden with some heavy load till he could carry it no longer, pulled and dragged about, and at last exposed with all his wounds to the gaze of a rude multitude who came and jeered him, what would be our feelings? Let us in our mind think of this person or that and consider how we should be overwhelmed and pierced through and through by such a hideous occurrence.
>
> But what is all this to the suffering of holy Jesus, which we bear to read of as a matter of course? Only think of Him, when in His wounded state, and without a garment on, He had to creep up the ladder, as He could, which led Him up the Cross high enough for His murderers to nail Him to it; and consider *who* it was that was in that misery . . .[9]

129

James Anthony Froude, looking back from agnostic old age and recalling a sermon on a similar theme, remembered that 'it was as if an electric stroke had gone through the church, as if every person present understood for the first time the meanings of what he had all his life been saying'. For Froude the electrifying sentence had been, 'Now I bid you recollect that He to whom these things were done was Almighty God'.[10] But for me the climax of the sermon I have just quoted is far more characteristic of the man: 'And consider *who* it was that was in that agony.' He does not tell us. This has all the restraint and allusiveness of Newman's customary manner. In his opening remarks about the kindly old mentor who is being tortured and buffeted we might have been tempted to suppose that he was thinking of Keble, but his mind was on the Ancient of Days.

The prose of the sermons perfectly matches their purpose. It is luminously clear. It is unshowy. Its musical effects sometimes depend upon the catalogue or the repetition.

> We are among men and we know that we are. We feel cold and hunger; we know what sensible things remove them. We eat, drink, clothe ourselves, dwell in houses, converse and act with others, and perform the duties of social life; and we feel vividly that we are doing so, while we do so. Such is our relation to one part of the innumerable beings which lie around us . . . And yet in spite of this universal world which we see, there is another world, quite as far-spreading, quite as close to us, and more wonderful; another world all around us, though we see it not, and more wonderful than the world we see . . .[11]

It was to bring this other world alive that Newman devoted himself in his sermons, preaching every week for a decision on the part of his hearers, to abandon materialism and sensuality and to inhabit that other world which he conjures up. 'I thought life might be a dream and I an angel . . .' Reading him, we think so too.

The great imaginative artist is one who can convey us into a wholly distinctive world, thereby changing, to some degree or another, the way in which we perceive things, or ourselves. In the post-Romantic age, the distinctiveness of an artist is one of the things we most treasure: the knowledge that this violin sonata is not merely sublime in itself but could have been composed by no one but Bartok; that this chair is Vincent Van Gogh's chair and this London Dickens's London.

The cluster of phenomena in the history of taste which involved the nineteenth century in its various flirtations with medievalism throws up some strange case histories in which the romantic ego is oddly at war with its own aesthetic purposes. An analogy with painting suggests itself. In the medieval church, the painter just as much as the stone-masons, the architects, the wood-carvers, and glass-makers, was an anonymous craftsman. His patrons would not have thanked him, as a modern patron might do, for depicting religious scenes from an imaginative new angle, or for stamping his own personality on the work. In short, they would not have thanked him for having a style. We are not supposed to exclaim, before a Madonna of the *trecento*, on the brilliant individualism of Duccio, though we might admire his superior craftsmanship. Nineteenth-century painters who absorbed the Ruskinian ethos or who were influenced by the Pre-Raphaelite Brotherhood were seeking in part to recapture this selfless absorption in colour and form, but few ever achieved it. Even Dyce, who is the best parodist of early renaissance painting, has an immediately recognizable personal manner. As for Holman Hunt, we can descry his garishly repellent canvases at a hundred yards. The same is true of the architects. True medieval Gothic lacks personality. But no trained eye could confuse Pearson with Butterfield, Pugin with Street.

Strachey identified Newman as 'a child of the Romantic revival', and also as one 'who could not withstand the last enchantment of the Middle Age'.[12] And we find in Newman's pages, particularly in his sermons, a similar struggle between Romantic egotism and a truly medieval spirit of anonymity. We believe R W Church when he said that Newman's sermons 'made men think of the things which the preacher spoke of, and not of the sermon or preacher'.[13] Equally we know that J A Froude was right to say that these sermons were 'the records of Newman's own mental experience'.

There is very little 'fine writing' in Newman's sermons, of the kind we might underscore in, say, Ruskin's *Stones of Venice*. Nor is there the wild eccentricity which Carlyle cultivated in his prose style. The electrifying quality of the *Parochial and Plain sermons* is partly achieved by their plainness. They present the strongest possible themes – the passion of Christ, the certainty of a future judgement – in the cool rational prose of an English gentleman. This effect is studied, not accidental, and their power stems, as Froude saw, from the fact that every word of them is a personal testimony. Newman does not place himself front stage in the sermons, but we are left in no doubt as we read them (how much more would this have been the case if we had heard them) that the drama of the Christian life is his own personal drama. In the subtlest, and we might say the politest, way he woos us with his silvery charm.

'Dreaming is not a fiction, but a real state of mind, and though only one or two in the whole world ever dreamed; and if these one or two or a dozen men spoke to the rest of the world, and unanimously witnessed to the existence of that mysterious state, many doubtless would resist their report, as they do the mysteries of the Gospel, on the grounds of its being unintelligible . . .'[14]

The effect of the sermons is therefore less like looking at a medieval painting and more like reading one of the great Romantic poets. We want to share in the drama. More, while the effect of the rhetoric lasts, we do share in it.

In his lectures to the Catholic University of Dublin in 1858, twenty years after his prodigious career as an Oxford preacher, Newman revealed how deeply and intelligently he had weighed the questions of literary style.

'Literature', he tells us, 'is of a personal character; it consists in the enunciations and teachings of those who have a right to speak as representatives of their kind, and in whose words their brethren find an interpretation of their own sentiments, a record of their own experience, and a suggestion for their own judgments.'[15]

The good writer, for Newman, is one who 'always has the right word for the right idea and never a word too much'. There are two types of style, using the word in its pejorative sense, which he rejects, and we could call them the decorative and the idiosyncratic. He wants, in other words, to be neither Walter Pater nor Thomas Carlyle. As an example of the first, he instances those Persians who pay professional writers to compose letters on their behalf. 'The man of thought comes to the man of words and the man of words, duly instructed in the thought, dips the pen of desire into the ink of devotedness and proceeds to spread it over the page of desolation. Then the nightingale of affection is heard to warble to the rose of loveliness, while the breeze of anxiety plays around the brow of expectation. This is what the Easterns', he adds with very English distaste, 'are said to consider fine writing.'[16]

The parody shows that if he had chosen, Newman could have

been a Walter Pater to a generation before the aesthetic movement began. Equally he rejects those idiosyncratic stylists who are 'guilty of the absurdity of making sentences at the very end of their literary labour'. As an example of this, he gives Samuel Johnson much as he loves 'the personal character and intellectual vigour' of the Great Cham. 'His style often outruns the sense and the occasion, and is wanting in that simplicity which is the attribute of genius.'[17] Style in Newman's consideration should be an expression of the man. Those who suppose that it is a mere decoration, or an elaboration of thoughts which could have been expressed in some other way, in some rhetoric which could have been learnt as in the schools of Alexandria or Isfahan, have failed to understand why we appreciate our great writers. 'Can they really think', Newman asks, 'that Homer, or Pindar, or Shakespeare, or Dryden, or Walter Scott, were accustomed to aim at diction for its own sake, instead of being inspired with their subject, and pouring forth beautiful words because they had beautiful thoughts?'[18]

It is interesting that he wrote these words five years before he wrote the *Apologia*. They contain the clue to the Newman magic, which was only to come to full flower in his autobiography. He did not know how true the words were of himself, because he had not written the book of which they are the supreme description. The style which he had evolved and which was so eloquently demonstrated in the Dublin lectures – the book which was to become *The Idea of a University* – was rich, mature, musical without being orotund, personal while never degenerating into mannerism or eccentricity. It is difficult to define a style, particularly a style like Newman's which is so perfectly the expression of a mind, a mind which is such a paradoxical mixture of bigoted strictness and personal tenderness, intellectual obliquity and emotional fervour, high intelligence and blind devotion. Musical analogies recur when one attempts the definition. A trivial example came to me when I was working on the script of a television programme about Newman and wished to quote the end of Part Six of the *Apologia*: 'On the morning of the 23rd I left the Observatory. I have never seen Oxford since, excepting its spires, as they are seen from the railway.' It may be supposed that they are two very ordinary sentences, but they are perfect, as in the preceding paragraph with its famously moving allusion to the snapdragons of Trinity. Now, part of the effect of the ending of the *Apologia* – and the end of Part Six is actually the ending of the story in narrative terms – is the brilliantly economical way that Newman whisks us back to the beginning of the story, just as it reaches its brutal end. For the previous two hundred pages we have entered into his reasons for being in love with Oxford. And then the friends come to say goodbye to him. And then he remembers the snapdragons which grew opposite his freshman's rooms, which he had taken as 'the emblem of my own perpetual residence even unto death in my university'. And then he is gone. And we know that nigh on twenty years have passed and he has never seen the place since, 'excepting its spires, as they are seen from the railway'. And the railway is a wonderful touch, because it makes us realize that inviolate Oxford, last enchantment of the Middle Ages, is now a distant scene, glimpsed by a heartbroken old man as he rattles up and down between Birmingham and London by a modern mode of transport. Its pathos is cinematic and it is done in so few words. That is partly why it is so moving. But it is also – and this is why I mention the television programme – a matter of music. The producer of the programme, anxious to keep the story as simple as possible, and aware that there might, conceivably, be people watching the programme who had never been to Oxford, suggested that mention of the Observatory was merely confusing. All that the viewer needed to be told was that Newman had left Oxford. It did not matter where he had spent his last night. So, as broadcast, the sentence read, 'On the morning of the 23rd, I left. I have never seen Oxford since, excepting its spires as they are seen from the railway.'

The sentence makes perfectly good sense, but it is no longer a Newman sentence. It lacks all musicality. I almost wanted to read it, if the Observatory could not be mentioned, 'On the morning of the 23rd, I left tum te-tum-titty' . . . because without those syllables, 'the Observatory', the sentence would be like a phrase of a violin sonata from which, for reasons of split-second timing, a recording studio had chosen to eliminate two or three notes. All Newman's writings, even the letters, are as finely woven as this. They seem luminous, even colourless, as far as idiosyncrasy of style is in question, until you try the experiment of removing or changing a few words. Then you realize that the sentences actually make a hypnotic music and that they sing in the head. They are memorable as great poetry is memorable, even though they are not great poetry. They are in the best as well as the worst sense of the word seductive.

Hundreds of examples could be chosen. Think of the lilting balance, and incidentally of the strange ambivalence, of Newman's contrast, again in the *Idea of the University*, between clever people losing their faith and uneducated people gaining it. Many believers must have read this passage and wondered which side Newman was on, since it is surely unnecessary for the purposes of argument that religious people here should be 'uneducated'. First, the doubters:

> Their eyes are opened, and like the judgment-stricken king in the tragedy, they see two suns, and a magic universe, out of which they look back upon their former state of faith and innocence with a sort of contempt, as if they were then but fools, and the dupes of imposture.

> On the other hand, religion has its own enlargement, and enlargement not of tumult, but of peace. It is often remarked of uneducated persons, that on their turning to God, looking into themselves, regulating their hearts, reforming their conduct, and meditating on death and judgment, heaven and hell, they seem to become in point of intellect, different beings from what they were. Before, they took things as they came, and thought no more of one thing than another. But now every event has a meaning: they have their own estimate of whatever happens to them, they are mindful of times and seasons and compare the present with the past: and the world, no longer dull, no longer monotonous, unprofitable and hopeless, is a various and complicated drama, with parts and an object, and an awful moral.[19]

As with my earlier example, the passage about leaving the Observatory, you could extract the same sense from this passage with drastic shortening, and a removal of adjectives. You would thereby destroy its effectiveness as a piece of writing, and it is one of Newman's finest pieces of writing.

Why is he important, not merely as a figure in church history, but in the history of English literature? Or, if we do not want to put the question in that way, in what does his excellence as a writer consist? After all, the world is full of sermons, and sermons do not normally concern the literary historian. Nor do treatises on education. And though Newman's *Idea of a University* is one of his best books, it disturbs and excites us least when he is talking about universities, and most when he turns aside to talk of this other matter, the interior drama which is taking place within the soul of a human being. This, I would contend, is his great theme as a writer, and the subject which he has made peculiarly his own.

It is a hundred years since he died, and in this centenary year there will be more who are inclined to praise Newman than to bury him. We shall hear much of his excellence as a philosopher, as a theologian, as an historian, as a controversialist. There might even be those – and perhaps that is what I was supposed to be doing today – who will sing his praises as a novelist and a poet. Just supposing, however, that this were not the case. Supposing that it were universally admitted that he was not much of a poet, nor a novelist. Supposing it were thought that there is something a bit dog-eared about dead ecclesiastical controversies, and that in a suffering universe, common sense must make us realize that it does not make a ha'penny worth of difference whether we are Anglicans or Roman Catholics.

I am not making these judgements myself. I am asking whether, if such judgements were made, they would destroy Newman's importance as a writer. And I would suggest that even if all these were conceded, Newman's reputation would hardly suffer at all. When I read his pages, I hear the clear authentic voice of an analytical and introspective mind who is able to describe what religion is, what it actually is. He is able to describe from the inside what it is like to see the world as 'a various and complicated drama with parts and an object and an awful moral'. Most religious people, writing in English prose, have never paused to do this. It may be that words fail them, or that they take it all for granted, or that they are so anxious to convert other people to their own point of view that they do not reflect on the singularity of what it is like to have that point of view; they do not describe, still less come to terms with what Newman, in one of his sermons, calls 'the mysteriousness of our present being'.

As the nineteenth century rolls by and the sea of faith ebbs out, nearly all the articulate and imaginative writers, together with the most distinguished intellects, would seem to have abandoned religious belief. Tennyson and Arnold can share with us the wistfulness of being half-believers. Harriet Martineau and George Eliot can tell us what it is like to lose faith altogether, and the aching void which it leaves in the heart, as it left voids in the hearts of J A Froude, Darwin, Huxley, Carlyle, Herbert Spencer, Leslie Stephen and so many others. Of those conspicuously intelligent men and women who continued to believe few were writers, and few were able to articulate not why they believed, but what it was like. Gladstone's diaries, for example, are just catalogues. They tell us absolutely nothing of what it was like to be that fascinatingly divided but committed and religious man. And who could ever guess what it was like to be, from the inside, Dr Pusey? Fairly peculiar, one might suppose.

Newman is able to focus with peculiar luminosity on the religious faculty within himself, which is why his *Apologia Pro Vita Sua* will always remain such an important and interesting book. It was also, as we know so well, an intensely painful book to write. He stood at his desk in Birmingham, often in floods of tears, as he dashed it off. The sentences of the opening pages have the jerkiness of sobs, and we may believe that he thought he was being truthful when he wrote them.

> It is not pleasant for me to be egotistical; nor to be criticised for being so. It is not pleasant to reveal to high and low, young and old, what has gone on within me from my early years. It is not pleasant to be giving to every shallow and flippant disputant the advantage over me of knowing my most private thoughts, I might even say the intercourse between myself and my Maker. But I do not like to be called to my face a liar and a knave. Nor should I be doing my duty to my faith or to my name were I to suffer it.

Kingsley's bluff lack of tact and his victim's preternatural touchiness are the chemical ingredients which call forth the most interesting book which Newman ever wrote.

As a religious treatise, the *Apologia* must be one of the most paradoxical documents in the history of the world. It describes how Newman came to an unequivocal faith in the Roman Catholic religion: that is, that religion is a revealed truth, that the incarnate God entrusted to a particular and recognizable institution on this earth the task of baptizing and teaching all nations. The whole point of being a Roman Catholic is that these large claims are received; religious truth, for adherents to such a system, as for the Moslems or the Mormons, is an objective thing, given to the faithful by the institution and not worked out for themselves.

Yet, as every page of the *Apologia* makes clear, Newman was guided by something more mysterious than argument. His reasons for accepting the authority of Rome seem individualistic and in this sense Protestant. 'Truth', as Kierkegaard was writing at about the same time, 'lies in subjectivity.' Though the book traces with such exactitude all the minutiae of those Oxford quarrels of the 1830s, the exact point at which Newman changed his mind about the Real Presence, his scrupulousness about avoiding the invocation of saints, and so forth, he disarmingly admits that these are not really matters in which the intellect plays a very important part. 'For myself, it was not logic which carried me on; as well might one say that the quicksilver in the barometer changes the weather. It is the concrete being that reasons; pass a number of years, and I find my mind in a new place; how? the whole man moves; paper logic is but the record of it.'[20]

I have already quoted at too great length from Newman's works, or I should feel tempted to quote entire, as J A Froude does in his masterly essay on 'The Oxford Counter-Reformation', that splendid passage towards the close of the *Apologia* in which Newman states that, 'If I looked into a mirror and did not see my face, I should have the sort of feeling which actually comes upon me, when I look into this living busy world, and see no reflexion of its Creator'.[21] He feels God within himself, but he cannot see him in the world of man. From its earliest pages, when he was a child who thought 'life might be a dream or I an angel' to the pious ending, Newman was writing about a subject which must always interest any thoughtful person, that is the religious faculty, the religious appetites of men and women.

It is as strong and as universal as the sexual appetite, and we have not said anything about it if we merely posit that the one appetite derives from the other. Whatever our individual *beliefs*, or non-beliefs, most of us are aware that we have a religious sensibility, but in the tradition of English literature it is not much explored. Had the gig, on the fateful morning, gone to Dover and had the young Newman crossed the Channel, he might have found himself at home in the traditions which nurtured Renan and Proust. Had Mr Newman been born in Petersburg, rather than in London, Newman might not have been such a literary fish out of water, for the Russians are fascinated by our religious sensibility and their best novelists have always written as openly about it as D H Lawrence wrote about sex. Newman's religious temperament was highly developed – for some Laodicean readers, disconcertingly so – but in English a religious mind has seldom been gifted with such a capacity for self-description. In the English language, I know no author except Wordsworth who can match him in this particular field, and few to rival him as a prose stylist. But then, I am drunk with the Newman music, and even when my mind moves in a direction directly opposite to his own; even when the particular matters which distressed or excited him seem to me as distressing or exciting as the controversies of Tweedle-dum and Tweedle-dee; even when his hysterical assaults on Liberalism make me glad to be, in his terms, a Liberal, I warm to him, and feel, as did those enthralled undergraduates in St Mary's during the 1830s, the strength and charm of the man.

NOTES

1. Joseph Butler, *Fifteen Sermons* (SPCK 1970), sermon 7, 16; p. 71.
2. Lytton Strachey, *Eminent Victorians* (Penguin 1948): 'Cardinal Manning', ch. 2, p. 23.
3. ibid., ch. 3, p. 36.
4. *Apologia* (Sheed & Ward 1976), p. 1.
5. F W Newman, *Phases of Faith* (6th edn, London, 1860; reprinted Leicester University Press 1970), p. 7.
6. *Loss and Gain* (Universe Books 1962), Part I, ch. vi, p. 22.
7. *Apologia*, ch. V, p. 160.
8. *Loss and Gain*, Part III, ch. xi, p. 245.
9. *Parochial and Plain Sermons* (San Francisco, Ignatius Press, 1987), VII, 10, p. 1488.
10. 'The Oxford Counter-Reformation' in J A Froude, *Short Studies on Great Subjects* (Longmans 1899), vol. IV, p. 286. Even so he has not remembered the original with complete accuracy. Newman writes more effectively: 'Now I bid you consider that that Face, so ruthlessly smitten, was the Face of God himself' (*Parochial and Plain Sermons*, VI, 6, p. 1223).
11. *Parochial and Plain Sermons*, IV, 13, pp. 853, 852, with Newman's order reversed.
12. op. cit., p. 23.
13. R W Church, *The Oxford Movement* (University of Chicago Press 1970), p. 93.
14. *Parochial and Plain Sermons*, IV, 19, p. 910.
15. *The Idea of a University* (Indiana, University of Notre Dame Press, 1982), p. 219 (Lecture on Literature).

16. ibid., p. 209.
17. ibid., p. 213.
18. ibid., p. 210.
19. ibid., pp. 100–1 ('Knowledge viewed in relation to learning').
20. *Apologia*, ch. IV, p. 113.
21. ibid., ch. V, p. 162.

· 7 ·

Newman and the Idea of a University

ROY JENKINS

Throughout his life Newman showed a keen interest in education. One of his earliest disputes in Oriel was in fact not religious at all, but concerned the operation of the tutorial system within the College. After he became a Roman Catholic he was commissioned with the task of founding a Catholic university in Ireland as a counterpoise to Trinity College, Dublin, from which his co-religionists were excluded. The Idea of a University *seeks to express the ideals upon which he thought university education ought to be based. Since it is commonly regarded as the classic defence of a liberal education of the kind which Oxford has, at its best, always sought to embody, one could scarcely find a more fitting modern commentator than the present Chancellor of Oxford University, Lord Jenkins of Hillhead.*

I have found the preparation of this lecture one of the most formidable tasks I have ever undertaken, and am inclined to the view that my sense of cancellarian duty to the University – which I interpret as meaning that I should not refuse a serious engagement which it is physically possible for me to fulfil – has led me to take leave of my senses. A few months ago I knew little about Newman, beyond the facts he was a Trinity undergraduate, an Oriel Fellow in the years when that college led the awakening from the Oxford slumber of the eighteenth century, and Vicar of St Mary's. I had some vague knowledge of his part in the launching of the Oxford Movement and of his retreat to Littlemore.

Forty years ago, now nearly a third of the time back to his sojourn there I addressed an election meeting in the Anglican schoolroom at Littlemore, but got little response from the small and stolid audience for what I hoped was my felicitous reference to their former parish priest. I think I would have got the correct year for his conversion to Rome, but I was hazy about the exact date of his move to Birmingham, although during my long years as an MP for the other end of that city I was aware of the presence of the Oratory and the church of St Philip Neri and of their Newman connection. I knew that Pope Leo XIII had shown that he was not Pope Pius IX by making Newman a cardinal, and I thought that was a good thing, rather like Cinderella being taken to the ball, and one in the eye for Cardinal Manning, although Manning, whatever else he was, was neither ugly nor a sister. I had read *Apologia Pro Vita Sua* as a very young man, and had found it surprisingly easy going. But that was about it.

I therefore found myself committed to spend a lot of time immersed in Newman, in the Discourses which make up *The Idea of a University* in particular, and in the circumstances in which they were delivered and/or composed. This concentration left a number of impressions, some of them contradictory, upon my mind. First (a blinding truism) that Newman was a man of exceptional interest. There seems to me to be more room for argument about his piety, although I would hesitate to pronounce on that, his charity, his simple niceness, or even his modesty, than about his fascination. This stems partly from his brilliance as a stylist (even though his imagery could be lush and his use of words was rarely economical), as an ironist, and as a polemicist. But it was more than that. He could write dull passages, sometimes I feel almost intentionally so, because he was getting round a corner in his argument with which he did not feel wholly at ease. But whether or not it was intentional he was certainly conscious that he had written a relatively dull passage. You can almost feel him waiting in slack water, hardly moving his paddle, yet preparing to swoop into the next stage of the argument as soon as a favourable current developed.

He had star quality, as surely as, amongst his contemporaries, did Gladstone or Tennyson or Carlyle. It is possible to confuse Keble with Pusey, or Pusey with Keble, and to wonder which was doing what at a particular time. It is never possible to confuse Newman with anyone. It is possible to be irritated or to be muddled by Newman, but very difficult to be bored by him. This is the more striking because I felt throughout that Newman's *mentalité* (my excuse for using the French rather than the English word is that I fondly imagine it to embrace not only the working of his own mind but also the intellectual climate in which he operated) is an ocean away not only from my own but from that of almost anyone, inside or outside the University, with whom I have frequent contact.

In Oxford the 1990 centenary celebrations culminated with a service in the University Church of St Mary's, at which the Archbishop of Canterbury was the preacher. It was a notable occasion, but I doubt if any service can recapture the atmosphere in which Newman, having slipped across the cobbled and trafficless High from Oriel, or in later days having walked in from Littlemore, and then, in Matthew Arnold's words, already quoted in an earlier contribution but well up to repetition, 'after gliding in the dim afternoon light through the aisles [of St Mary's and] rising into the pulpit, in the most entrancing of voices [broke] the silence with words and thoughts which were a religious music – subtle, sweet, mournful'.[1] Yet we know from Gladstone, among others, that Newman's 'sermons were read, with hardly any change in the inflexion of the voice and without any gesture on the part of the preacher, whose eyes remained fixed on the text in front of him'.[2] The two descriptions are only superficially incompatible and whatever was or was not the histrionic quality of Newman's sermons there was a still more remarkable quality about the later ones, and that was their capacity to excite and divide the University. What would the Vice-Chancellor think? Would the Regius Professor of Divinity retaliate? What would the Heads of Houses do? How might the Provost of Oriel navigate between his peers and his turbulent Fellow? Would Convocation censure Tract Ninety, which was a Newman sermon in print, or would dedicated Tractarian Proctors, as happened in February 1845, veto the censure being put to the vote? What would be done by poor Bishop Bagot of Oxford, a High Church sympathizer, who liked a quiet life and found himself presiding over the cockpit of whether or not Anglicanism could be Catholicism.

Even the Duke of Wellington, as Chancellor of the University, and the last who was not himself an Oxonian, could not remain entirely remote from these quivering controversies. In the mid-thirties he had inclined to the High Church side, at least to the extent of being hostile to R D Hampden, another member of the Oriel constellation of *circa* 1820, Melbourne's nominee as Regius Professor of Divinity. But he soon thought the Tractarians went too far in trying to torment Hampden. Schism was the great evil, he admonished the Vice-Chancellor, worse even than heresy or impiety. And by 1844 Wellington was determined, to the brink of threatening resignation, that his nomination of the Evangelical Warden Symons of Wadham as the new Vice-Chancellor, should be accepted. The Tractarians forced a vote, but were overwhelmingly defeated in the Sheldonian, and Wellington responded to this victory with suitable lack of magnanimity by announcing that he would never allow such a vote again. The power of the Chancellor to nominate the Vice-Chancellor is now temporarily in abeyance, but I have found looking into these matters very instructive.

All this was well past and it was nearly nine years since Newman had last entered St Mary's and six years since he had seen Oxford, except from the railway, when he went to Dublin in May 1852 and delivered on five successive Monday afternoons the lectures which became the first half of *The Idea of a University*. He records at the end – a sympathetic thought to me today – that they 'have oppressed me more than anything else of the kind in my life'.[3] However he did not allow this to put him in a compromising mood towards his audience. Ladies, to his surprise it appears, had been present. But he did not pay too much attention to them and wrote: 'I *fancied* a slight sensation in the room when I said, not Ladies and Gentlemen, but Gentlemen.'[4] However, this may have owed less to a sense of affront at female presence, although Newman was certainly capable of feeling that, than to the fact that he constantly employed the word 'gentlemen' as a sort of alpenstock to lever him up the hill of an important stage in his argument. Perhaps it was to remind himself of the difference between delivering a lecture and preaching a sermon. Indeed he carried it to the almost ludicrous extent of spattering the texts of the last few Discourses, which were never publicly delivered but form to my mind the more interesting half of the whole, with this form of address.

The five delivered lectures themselves were a considerable on-the-spot success. They were listened to by high quality attendances of about four hundred, and Newman was delighted with the quick perception of the Irish audience just as they were with the distinction of the lecturer and the elevation of his thought. This was as well, for the book for which they were written, which Newman called 'one of my two most perfect works, artistically'[5] (a strong statement for any author), attracted much less critical notice and much smaller sales than his previous recent works. By contrast its long-term resonance has been enormous, so much so that it has become impossible to dissociate from Newman the evocative phrase – *The Idea of a University*. John Sparrow made some attempt in his 1965 Cambridge Clark lectures to divert it on to Mark Pattison, who had a more solid influence in nineteenth-century university life than did Newman, but who lacked his capacity to arouse excitement. But Warden Sparrow, who allowed Newman, together with Matthew Arnold, a status equal to Pattison in the relevance to contemporary problems of his mid-Victorian pronouncements on universities, did not succeed in his diversionary attempt. Pattison stands with Jowett as one of the two dominating Heads of Houses of the second half of the nineteenth century, but 'the idea of a university' belongs to Newman, even though he never set foot in the only university which he understood between 1846 and 1877, between the ages of 45 and 76, which was by any standards a substantial and significant segment of his life.

The circumstances of his Dublin sojourn were unfavourable from a number of points of view. Just over a year earlier the Roman Catholic hierarchy in Britain, with its panoply of territorial bishops, had been established. Newman was unenthusiastic. He thought seminaries and education were more important than sees. But he was far too new a convert to be able to protest, even though he bore some of the brunt of the reaction against what was widely regarded as aggressive Catholic presumption. The Achilli case in which he was prosecuted for criminal libel against an unfrocked Dominican, who had subsequently been taken up by the Evangelical Alliance and had toured the country denouncing the corruption of Rome, is one of the most curious and ill-fitting episodes in Newman's life. In a Birmingham lecture in the summer of 1850 Newman had drawn, without checking, on an anonymous pamphlet in fact written by Bishop Wiseman, later Cardinal Archbishop of Westminster, which denounced the personal immorality of which Achilli had been convicted by a papal court in Rome. Achilli, with his Low Church sponsors, got Newman indicted. The evidence which was essential for his defence was constantly on the point of arrival from Rome, but in spite of a special mission by two Birmingham Oratorians, it was never there when it was needed.

There was a series of portentous court hearings before the very anti-Catholic Chief Justice, Lord Campbell. It must have been a great *cause célèbre*. Newman's counsel, as was permissible in those days of private fees for Government law officers, was the Attorney-General, Cockburn, who was later to be Chief Justice himself and to achieve fame by inventing the definition of obscenity as 'a tendency to deprave or corrupt those into whose hands [the complained of publication] may fall' which subsequently stood for ninety years. Cockburn was almost as full of anti-Catholic prejudices as Campbell, and only attempted to defend Newman by holding the complained of passage like a piece of soiled linen in his finger-tips. In Dublin in 1852 Newman thought that the main hearing would come on at any moment, and faced the real prospect of imprisonment for a year or so. On 24 June the verdict was given against him, but the sentence for which he had to wait another seven months, was only a fine of £100 (the equivalent of about £4000 today), which led Newman's supporters to proclaim, almost as though he were a modern Sunday newspaper editor, that the result was a moral victory. But all this lay heavy on his mind in Dublin. In addition he was barely settled into the new Oratory in Edgbaston. To deal with these concerns he made the inconvenient journey across St George's Channel and by the new railway between Birmingham and Holyhead several times during the series.

More important, however, was the fact that Newman had embarked on a largely impossible task in Ireland. In 1851 he had accepted an invitation from Archbishop (later Cardinal) Cullen of Armagh to become founding Rector of a Catholic University in Ireland. Cullen, after many years in Rome, where he had developed an authoritarian cast of mind, had returned to Ireland only in 1849, and had been appointed apostolic delegate for the foundation of the University. He was to be translated to the see of Dublin in 1852, which meant that he had still more opportunity to interfere with Newman's plans, although not apparently to reply to his letters. And he was interested only in the new University providing a strictly religious education. He attended at least some of Newman's lectures, but he must have regarded them as containing a good deal of froth, some of it dangerous.

The position was even more complicated than that. There were also two powerful factions in the Irish hierarchy (and Newman was in some sense responsible to the bishops as a whole) which diverged from Cullen in contrary directions. Archbishop Murray of Dublin (until 1852) was attracted by the London government's scheme for Queen's Colleges (one of which, in Belfast, has survived both in fact and in name, and two of which, in Cork and Galway, have survived under different names), which would be open equally to Catholics and Protestants. And Archbishop MacHale of Tuam wanted an Irish Nationalist University, 'a Fenian college', as those of a different view, including Cullen and Murray, might have described it.

And what did Newman want? Essentially, he wanted a Catholic Oxford on the banks of the Liffey. And the Catholicism, while it was to infuse its heart, was not to be restrictive of the movement of the limbs, as Dr Cullen might have wished. Nor really was the Dublin location important to Newman. Outside the city might have been better, outside Ireland would have done had the papal authority not been given for a *Catholic University in Ireland.* Newman was free of much nineteenth- (and twentieth-) century educated English Catholic impatience with the Irish, but he was not much interested in Irish nationalism, and certainly not in a nationalist university. He wanted his university to be for anglophone Catholics, for England as much as for Ireland. (I am not sure he embraced the thought of America.) And he wanted it to be a university for gentlemen. In Discourse VIII he came very near to saying that gentlemanliness was next to godliness. Admittedly he defines (or rather describes) gentlemanliness in a peculiarly self-effacing way. After stating 'that it is almost a definition of gentleman to say he is one who never inflicts pain',[6] he goes into a famous description of high but gentle good manners.

In Discourse V, however, he gives a more succinct account of the relation of gentlemanliness both to a liberal education and to religion:

Liberal Education makes not the Christian, not the Catholic, but the gentleman. It is well to be a gentleman, it is well to have a cultivated intellect, a delicate taste, a candid, equitable, dispassionate mind, a noble and courteous bearing in the conduct of life; – these are the connatural qualities of a large knowledge; they are the objects of a University; I am advocating, I shall illustrate and insist upon them; but still they are no guarantee for

147

sanctity or even for conscientiousness, they may attach to the man of the world, to the profligate, to the heartless . . .[7]

Yet for all Newman's stress on self-effacement and his insistence that refinement is not saintliness (although it 'may set off and recommend an interior holiness just as the gift of eloquence sets off logical argument'), he leaves us in no doubt that it is not rough diamonds with hearts of gold or 'nature's gentlemen' that he is talking about. It is those who have acquired their urbanity through the traditional processes of a privileged liberal education. In 1856 he put it even more sharply when he wrote that he had gone to Dublin because 'the Holy See had decided that Dublin was to be the place for Catholic education of the upper classes in these Islands . . .'[8]

So the conflicts between the desires of the different sponsors, and between aspiration and what was realistically possible, pile up. Newman wanted an idealized version of collegiate life under the dreaming spires, undefiled by the Reformation, trans-shipped to Leinster. And he wanted it to be filled with devoutly Catholic young men who combined the Whig virtues of an easy-going and cultured tolerance with the Tory virtues of a natural acceptance of authority and revealed truth. But neither economically nor sociologically was there room for a Christ Church on St Stephen's Green, within a quarter of a mile of Trinity moreover, and Archbishop Cullen would not have dreamt of letting him have it even had it been practicable. And to compound the contradictions much of Newman's thought was conditioned by the pluralism of Oxford, while the minds of others and the constitution with which he had to work were much more influenced by the model of the centralized and professorially controlled Catholic University of Louvain in Belgium.

In the circumstances what seem to me remarkable are not the considerable disappointments but that the scheme was not a more dramatic failure than it was. Newman survived in Dublin for six and a half years from the date of his 1852 lectures. For only four of them was he formally Rector, and there were frequent absences in Birmingham because he gave at least an equal priority to the affairs of the Oratory, which was another cause of dissension with Cullen. He established a house with about ninety students in the heart of Dublin, and indeed a University Church, with the somewhat disproportionate capacity of 1200. And the Catholic University as such survived until 1882, and then left substantial educational legacies, of which perhaps the most considerable has been the medical school, which could be regarded as ironical in view of the secondary role to which Newman relegated vocational education.

To what extent was Newman irrevocably Oxford-conditioned, even when he had spread a trail of intellectual and liturgical upheaval in the University and spent long years as exiled from the city as the Scholar Gipsy? It was I think the author of the preceding contribution, A N Wilson, who aroused in my mind the Scholar Gipsy thought with his evocative television portrait in autumn 1989 which left me with the loose impression of Newman haunting the Cumnor Hills and looking down with ineffable sadness at a Turneresque view of the Oxford skyline.

On the other hand, I T Ker, Newman's 1988 biographer, wrote that it was 'leaving Littlemore, unlike leaving Oxford or St Mary's, [which was] very painful for Newman'.[9] It was part of Newman's fascination that he was frequently capable of unexpected judgements about places, as about people. He would be as good an example as one could possibly imagine of a figure who was quintessentially Oxonian rather than Cantabrigian. Yet, when he first saw Cambridge, at the surprisingly late age of 31, he wrote, 'I do really think the place finer than Oxford'.[10] And when in 1846 he was on the most symbolically important journey to the Eternal City of any nineteenth-century person from England he perversely decided that Milan was 'a most wonderful place – to me more striking than Rome'.[11] He appears to have rated Milan Cathedral together with Trinity (Oxford) College Chapel – an unusual pair – as almost his favourite ecclesiastical buildings.

Yet, despite some unwillingness to worship at predictable shrines, I think Newman did carry a half visible Oxford canopy around with him for the forty-five years of his Roman Catholic life. In the Dublin Discourse VII for example, there is the panegyric of Oriel. It is worth citing at length for it is a typical, although by no means the most brilliant, example of Newman's cumulative style, by which he uses cascades of words to build up an idea like a range of hills with each summit rising a little higher than the previous one, but also steers through this mountain chain in order to get into position for the next axis of aggressive advance. I say 'aggressive' for I find it beyond dispute that Cardinal Newman, for all his portrait of that 'parfit gentil knight' which was his ideal of a gentleman, was a polemicist of an elegant deadliness which is met only once in a generation. The sole comparable figure in this respect that I have encountered in our recent university is Professor Hugh Trevor-Roper, who deserves his nobility as Lord Dacre even more for his sword than for his robe.

Newman's quarry in this early part of Discourse VII was no less a figure than John Locke. Newman had perhaps a keener sense of intellectual than of ecclesiastical hierarchy, and he knew that Locke was too strong a fortress to be attacked without a considerable preliminary investment. Lesser (although by no means negligible) figures like former Lord Chancellor Brougham or Bishop Mattly of Durham he would engage more directly. Even in these lesser cases, however, there is an aesthetic pleasure in watching Newman get into position for the attack. His old adversary Dr Arnold of Rugby could hardly have prepared for a flogging with more loving care than Newman does for an intellectual joust. Just as Arnold, while rolling up his sleeves, might have referred to the eminence of the boy's parents and the promise with which he came to the school, so Newman pays preliminary tribute to the general respect in which the right reverend prelate or the most learned lord is held and the lucidity with which he expresses his ideas; perhaps even (although not I think in the case of Brougham) to the probity of his personal life. Then comes the thrust, delivered like a matador's deadly lunge.

But Locke, almost as giant an Oxonian as Newton was a Cantabrigian one, could only be assaulted after a more elaborate approach march. So we have an eulogy of the recently dead Dr Copleston, Provost of Oriel in Newman's early days and later Bishop of Llandaff, and with him of John Davison, another member of the Oriel galaxy whose devastating attack on R L Edgeworth's fallacies on *Professional Education* was really, Newman says, an attack on the luminaries of the *Edinburgh Review* and behind them 'on a far greater author . . . who in a past age had argued on the same side'.[12] So the siege gun was at last in position for the engagement with Locke.

But in introducing his Irish and Catholic audience to 'the Protestant Bishop of Llandaff' Newman felt that he had a peg on which he could hang some of his feelings about Oriel, which had nurtured him for a quarter of a century but which he had not seen for nearly a decade. As a further convolution he does so sufficiently archly that the name of Oriel, as though it were that of a modest mistress, is never mentioned, and I was indeed far into the passage before I was certain which college he was talking about:

In the heart of Oxford there is a small plot of ground, hemmed in by public thoroughfares, which has been in the possession of and the house of one Society for about 500 years. In the old time of Boniface VIII and John XXII, in the age of Scotus and Occam and Dante, before Wyclif or Huss had kindled those miserable fires which are still raging to the ruin of the highest interests of man, an unfortunate King of England, Edward II, flying from the field of Bannockburn, is said to have made a vow to the Blessed Virgin to found a religious house in her honour . . .

The visitor, whose curiosity has been excited by its present fame, gazes perhaps with something of disappointment on a collection of buildings which have with them so few of the circumstances of dignity or wealth. Broad quadrangles, high halls and chambers, ornamental cloisters, stately walls, or umbrageous gardens, a throng of students, ample reserves or a glorious history, none of these things were the portion of that old Catholic foundation; nothing in short which to the common eye sixty years ago would have given tokens of what it was to be. But it had at that time a spirit working within it, which enabled its inmates to do, amid its seeming insignificance, what no other body in the place could equal.[13]

One of the things it did was to elect fellows solely on the basis of what Newman rather oddly described as 'public and patriotic grounds', and without regard not only to connection but to university class lists. One result was that Newman's disastrous schools results of 1820 were compensated for by his being elected a Fellow of Oriel sixteen months later. For this he remained grateful, but his feelings towards that college, in spite of some fluctuations in his years of crisis, were I think based on a more lively emotion than that of gratitude. Oriel's diversity of intellects and religious positions, as well as his memory of other colleges with broader quadrangles and more umbrageous gardens, infused much of his unrealistic hopes for what he might create in Dublin.

The Oriel passage I have dealt with at length not only to illustrate Newman's attitude to Oxford but also to exemplify both the circumlocutory and the rhetorical nature of his style. He was a great rhetorician. He was so in both the favourable and the less favourable sense of the word. He was certainly a persuasive and impressive speaker. But he was also given to the use of words more for ornamentation than for design. Disraeli's jibe about Gladstone, 'a sophistical rhetorician, inebriated with the exuberance of his own verbosity', could, with the word sophistical (which is not appropriate) left out, be applied just as well to Newman. His style is less portentous than Gladstone's. It reminds me more of Christopher Fry into whose plays in the 1940s and 1950s felicitous words tumbled like stars from a magnificent firework. Newman was moderately austere in the physical surroundings of life, but not in his use of words or imagery, where he was luxuriantly self-indulgent. He was as addicted to never using one word where ten words will do as Mr Kinnock is accused of being, although his phrases were incomparably better chosen.

An outstanding example is provided in Discourse I of *The Idea*, where Newman has to deal with the awkward fact that the Pope had laid it down that there must be a purely Catholic university. Newman makes no attempt to pretend that it is not awkward: 'It is the decision of the Holy See. St Peter has spoken, it is he who has enjoined that which seems to us so unpromising.'[14] He does not attempt to argue for this decision on its merits. Instead he asks for it to be accepted on the basis of the proven record of the papacy over 1800 years: 'He has spoken, and has a claim on us to trust him.' Newman then a little implausibly says, 'These are not the words of rhetoric, Gentlemen, but of history'; and then proceeds to sweep into a prose-poem of quasi-historical rhetoric which uses every possible evocative name and image not only to extol the early Christian cause but to bind England and Ireland together in a tradition of civilizing holiness.

> . . . the two islands . . . , in a dark and dreary age, were the two lights of Christendom . . . O memorable time, when St. Aidan and the Irish monks went up to Lindisfarne and Melrose, and taught the Saxon youth, and when a St. Cuthbert and a St. Eata repaid their charitable toil![15]

And so he continues for several hundreds of words, through the Christian exploits of Mailduf, and St Aldheim, and St Egbert, and St Willibrod, and 'the two noble Ewalds', to Alcuin 'the pupil of both the English and the Irish schools' who was sent for by

Charlemagne to 'revive science and letters in France'. 'Such was the foundation of the school of Paris, from which, over the course of centuries, sprang the famous University [which was] the glory of the middle ages.'

So the awkward decision was dissolved in this paean to Anglo-Irish partnership which elided encouragingly into the foundation of the great University of the Sorbonne. And the lecture concluded by saying that England and Ireland had changed but 'Rome is where it was, and St Peter is the same . . . And now surely he is giving us a like mission, and we shall become one again, while we zealously and lovingly fulfill it.'[16] If that is not rhetoric, I do not know what is.

Equally, at the end of Discourse IX, entitled 'The Duties of the Church Towards Knowledge', he ends with the most tremendous *tour de force* which owes more to oratory than to relevance. He is attempting first to sum up what he has previously said, which he is rarely good at, for his thoughts live in his phrases and fade when they are reduced to summary form. Second, he is attempting to reconcile his strong shafts of instinctive tolerance with his respect for the authority of the Church, and gets himself, perhaps only to my inadequately spiritual mind, into a very great muddle. He has just proclaimed a very firm libertarian doctrine on literature: 'I say, from the nature of the case, if Literature is to be made a study of human nature, you cannot have a Christian Literature. It is a contradiction in terms to attempt a sinless Literature of sinful man.'[17] And he adds, 'We would be shrinking from our plain duty, Gentlemen, did we leave out Literature from Education.' The University, he adds, is not to be a convent or even a seminary. 'It is a place to fit men of the world for the world.'[18]

But how is this to be reconciled with the authority of the Church over every aspect of this University. Is he advocating or defending such pervasive authority? In Discourse II he seems to be taking up a much more modest position in regard to Catholic authority: 'As to the range of University teaching certainly the very name of University is inconsistent with restrictions of any kind.'[19] In this Discourse he advances from this only to the limited claim that as theology is part of knowledge it cannot be excluded from the subjects taught at a true university. It is at least entitled to a chair (or chairs) amongst many. From there he proceeds to an intermediate position of refuting what he calls the Lutheran advocacy of the complete separation of science and religion. He postulates a modern philosopher of science asking him 'Why cannot you go your way and let us go ours?' and says: 'I answer, in the name of the Science of Religion, when Newton can dispense with the metaphysicians, then may you dispense with us.'[20] But he is still confining himself to an argument for the wholeness of knowledge and to religion's claim to a place in it.

Then in Discourse IX, quite close to the libertarian passage on literature, he suddenly goes much further:

> If the Catholic faith is true, a University cannot exist externally to the Catholic pale, for it cannot teach Universal Knowledge if it does not teach Catholic theology. That is certain, but still, though it had ever so many theological Chairs, that would not suffice to make it a Catholic University; for theology would be included in its teaching only as a branch of knowledge, only as one of many constituent portions, however important a one, of what I have called Philosophy. Hence a direct and active jurisdiction of the Church over it and in it is necessary, lest it should become the rival of the Church with the community at large in those theological matters which to the Church are exclusively committed . . .[21]

Much of the rest of this final Discourse, with the exception of the passage on literature, is Newman at his uneasiest. His words do not flow with their usual spontaneity. There are a great number of uses of 'Gentlemen' and 'that is certain', the latter always the most certain sign of Newman's uncertainty. And then suddenly he escapes from this viscosity by hitting on the idea of bringing the whole thing to an end by throwing everything into a panegyric of St Philip Neri, 'my own special Father and Patron', as he refers to him. It is like the finale of an open air concert I once attended which brought the 1812 Overture to a conclusion with cymbals bashing, cannons pounding, fireworks exploding and the conductor exhausting himself with enthusiasm:

> Nay, people came to him, not only from all parts of Italy, but from France, Spain, Germany and all Christendom, and even the infidels and Jews, who had ever any communication with him, revered him as a holy man. The first families of Rome, the Massimi, the Aldobrandini, the Colonnas, the Altieri, the Vitelleschi, were his friends and his penitents. Nobles of Poland, Grandees of Spain, Knights of Malta could not leave Rome

without coming to him. Cardinals, Archbishops and Bishops were his intimates, Federigo Borromeo haunted his room and got the name of Father Philip's soul. The Cardinal Archbishops of Verona and Bologna wrote books in his honour. Pope Pius IV died in his arms. Lawyers, painters, musicians, physicians, it was the same with them. Baronius, Zazzara, Ricci, left the law at his bidding, and joined his congregation to do its work, to write the annals of the Church, and to die in the odour of sanctity. Palestrina had Father Philip's ministrations in his last moments. Animuccia hung about him during life, sent him a message after death, and was conducted by him through Purgatory to Heaven. And who was he, I say all the while, but an humble priest, a stranger in Rome, with no distinction of family or letters, no claim of station or of office, great simply in the attraction with which a Divine Power had gifted him? And yet thus humble, thus unennobled, thus empty-handed, he has achieved the glorious title of Apostle of Rome.[22]

It was a magnificent extravaganza, even if veering at times towards being a Jennifer's Diary of life in sixteenth-century Rome, but it was hardly a satisfactory synthesis of the competing roles of liberal culture and religious authority in the scheme of an ideal university between which he had veered throughout the nine Discourses. The dust was stardust, but he was frankly throwing it into the eyes of his audience while he escaped under its cover from the dilemma into which he had put himself. When, therefore, the whole series came to an end, and the work to which it led was complete (only one paragraph after the end of this pyrotechnical exhibition) I was left dazzled but intellectually unsatisfied. Newman had mostly held me spellbound in the grip of his prose, but he had convinced me neither that he had a practical plan for an Irish university in the 1850s or that he had left guidelines of great relevance for a university of any nationality or any or no faith today.

This does not mean that he did not shine splendid shafts of light on to particular issues. I greatly enjoyed his attack on Victorian materialist values, where Nassau Senior, first Professor of Political Economy in this University, is set up with many compliments, both to his own eminence and to the 'unsordidness' of Oxford, to be the bull which is felled: '. . . the pursuit of wealth . . .' he exposes Senior as saying, 'is, to the mass of mankind, the great source of *moral* improvement . . .' 'I really should on every account be sorry, Gentlemen, to exaggerate, but indeed one is taken by surprise, one is startled, on meeting with so very categorical a contradiction of our Lord, St Paul, St Chrystostom, St Leo, and all Saints.'[23]

Equally firm was his rejection in Discourse VII, many years ahead of its time, of the principle of contract funding: 'Now this is what some great men are very slow to allow; they insist that Education should be confined to some particular and narrow end, and should issue in some definite work, which can be weighed and measured. They argue as if everything, as well as every person, had its price; and that where there has been a great outlay, they have a right to expect a return in kind.'[24]

Then again, there is his exhortation, in Discourse VI, against losing one's way in detail and specialization. He starts with a little text: 'A great memory does not make a philosopher, any more than a dictionary can be called a grammar.'[25] Soon afterwards he goes into a fine passage which expands the need to command facts from a hillock, a sort of 'Wellington at Waterloo' theory of knowledge.

> I say then, if we would improve the intellect, we must ascend . . . It matters not whether our field of operation be wide or limited; in every case, to command it, is to mount above it. Who has not felt the irritation of mind and impatience created by a deep rich country, visited for the first time, with winding lanes and high hedges, and green steeps, and tangled woods, and every thing smiling indeed, but in a maze? The same feeling comes upon us in a strange city, when we have no map of its streets. Have you not heard of practised travellers, when they come first into a place, mounting some high hill or church tower, by way of reconnoitring its neighbourhood. In like manner you must be above your knowledge, not under it, or it will oppress you; and the more you have of it, the greater will be the load.[26]

So Newman could have been expected to be pretty strong on all the main issues which beset universities today. He would have been against contract funding, he would have supported tenure and academic freedom, certainly against any depredations from the state and probably instinctively against any from Archbishop Cullen, although he would have found it more difficult to speak unequivocally about this. Student loans, I think, he would have found difficult to engage with, although he would not have been in favour of encouraging the pursuit of careers of mammon in order to repay. I am not sure that he told us much about how to strike the balance between research and the teaching of the young, although his emphasis was all on the latter. He respected science, but I do not think that he regarded the advancement of the frontiers of knowledge as the most important form of human activity, any more than he did the pursuit of wealth, and there can be no doubt that he would have been on the restrictive side in recent controversies about experiments with the embryo.

I agree with the view of Professor Owen Chadwick[27] that although Newman professed himself to have spent his life fighting liberalism, this was only true on his own very special and religious definition of liberalism which almost equated it with intellectual brashness, and that some of his work had a considerable liberalizing influence. Yet from the High Toryism of his outraged opposition to Catholic emancipation when he was a young Fellow of Oriel to his view when he was a very old man that issues should not be pursued when the results of the enquiry might unsettle 'simple people', he imposed restrictions upon himself which necessarily set a limit to seeing him as the patron saint of a university as a republic of ideas, as unfettered as it was broad-based.

I have written more about Newman and less about universities than you might have expected me to do. That is partly because I have many more opportunities to talk about universities than I do to talk about Newman, and partly because I have found him such a wholly absorbing even if sometimes tantalizing subject.

NOTES

1. M Arnold, 'Emerson' in *Discourses in America* (Macmillan 1885), pp. 139–40.
2. I T Ker, *John Henry Newman: A Biography* (Oxford, Clarendon Press, 1988), p. 91.
3. *Letters and Diaries*, ed. C S Dessain et al. (Oxford University Press 1973–84), XV, pp. 98–9.
4. LD XV, pp. 83–4.
5. LD XV, p. 226.
6. *The Idea of a University* (Indiana, University of Notre Dame Press, 1981), VIII, 10, p. 159.

7. *The Idea of a University*, V, 9, p. 91.
8. LD XVII, p. 178.
9. LD XVII, pp. 318–19.
10. LD III, p. 66.
11. LD XI, p. 249.
12. *The Idea of a University*, VII, 3, p. 120.
13. ibid., p. 117.
14. ibid., I, 5, p. 10.
15. ibid., I, 6 and 7, p. 13.
16. ibid., I, 7, p. 14.
17. ibid., IX, 7, p. 174.
18. ibid., IX, 8, pp. 176–7.
19. ibid., II, 1, p. 15.
20. ibid., III, 4, p. 39.
21. ibid., IX, 1, p. 163.
22. ibid., IX, 9, pp. 180–1.
23. ibid., IV, 12, p. 69.
24. ibid., VII, 2, pp. 115–16.
25. ibid., VI, 5, p. 102.
26. ibid., VI, 7, pp. 105–6.
27. O Chadwick, *Newman* (Oxford University Press 1983), ch. 7, pp. 71–6.

· 8 ·

An Ecumenical Perspective

ROBERT RUNCIE

In 1890 at Newman's funeral there was present only one Anglican dignitary, the then Dean of Durham. It is a measure of how far ecumenical relations have advanced that a century later when it came to organizing a service in the University Church at Oxford to celebrate the centenary of his death not only was the planning committee entirely ecumenical but so was the result, with both diocesan bishops (the Anglican Bishop of Oxford and the Roman Catholic Archbishop of Birmingham) agreeing to take part and no less a personage than the Archbishop of Canterbury himself agreeing to preach. During his occupancy of the see Dr Runcie has sought hard to foster improved relations between the Anglican and Roman Communions. In this sermon he indicates how a man who spent half his life in each Church can act as a guide for us to the future.

'For whoever would save his life will lose it and whoever loses his life for my sake and the gospel's will save it' (Mark 8.35).

This church is marked by the conflicts of Christendom. It bears the scars of those wounded in the house of friends. From here Thomas Cranmer went to his death. From here a former vicar Stephen Rousham went out to become a recusant priest and to be executed in Gloucester. John Wesley went out a man despised and rejected by a complacent eighteenth-century Oxford. John Henry Newman left this pulpit for exile in Littlemore. All these were, in their own way, men of conflict, signs of contradiction. All paid the price of suffering.

159

But now something of a miracle has happened. These heroes of our separate identities have become agents of reconciliation. A few years ago, an ecumenical celebration of the life of John Henry Newman would have been either impossible or an intolerable embarrassment. How is it that a man who once stirred such passions can now bring us together not just in common gratitude but also in pilgrimage towards that fulness of unity which is God's will?

If we follow Newman, he will surely lead us to the evangelical centre of our faith, to the Word made flesh, to Christ crucified and risen. When he occupied this pulpit he did not proclaim the manifesto of an ecclesiastical faction. He preached quietly and insistently, biblically, the gospel of Jesus Christ and called his hearers to conversion and holiness. 'I bid you consider that that face so ruthlessly smitten is the face of God himself.' For him, the struggle for faith was the struggle to preserve this central truth which was not man's opinion but God's word of love.

He was not an orator to inflame the mob or draw the crowds. St Mary's was rarely more than half full at 4 o'clock on Sunday afternoons when he preached. It was dinner hour in the Colleges and 'most men preferred a warm dinner without Newman's sermon to a cold one with it'. But to those who came he spoke as no other preacher of his time. The haunting voice *'touched into life old truths* . . . when he spoke of the "individuality of the soul", the "invisible world", or "the Church a home for the lonely". As he spoke, he laid his finger on some inner place in the hearer's heart, and told him things about himself he had never known till then.'[1] Those words were written by a Presbyterian. Even in his Oxford days, Newman could transcend divisions.

Newman's preaching changed when he became a Roman Catholic. It was not merely that he then began preaching, as was customary amongst Catholic priests, without a full script, but his sermons were less of law, more of grace. The struggle to affirm dogma – a characteristic of his Anglican preaching – is cast aside. Dogma is assumed. From that cradle of certainty Newman could afford to be more speculative in his thinking and preaching. The Church was the vehicle wherein God's grace could be seen at work in history.

That too can draw us together, for although the Christian community was thrown on the stream of history, Newman did not see it carried ever further away from primitive purity. He argued that religion became corrupt when it refused 'to follow the course of doctrine as it moves on'.[2] The way of heresy was found in arrested development, burying the gospel treasure in the ground rather than risking it in the mental currencies of the world. 'Such a risk must be undergone', he said, if the gospel is 'duly to be understood, and much more if it is to be fully exhibited.'[3] The gospel is God's Word, coming into the world, the incarnate Lord, who shows that God risks his identity in the stream of history. In the life of the Church the truth has again and again to be lived – 'Whoever would save his life will lose it; and whoever will lose his life for my sake and the gospel's will save it'.

The evangelical and apostolic Church, resting upon the once-for-all character of Christ's death and resurrection, is also the catholic Church moving into alien worlds and cultures to experience not a diminution of its identity, but an ever increasing enrichment. 'What I held in 1816, I held in 1833, and I hold in 1864. Please God I shall hold it to the end.'[4]

There is paradox here, but it is the paradox of a gospel in which God becomes man for our salvation. There was more paradox in Newman, some of it less attractive. He remained a controversialist. He was always sharp. He could be feline. He could be cruel, as when he said that the invalid wife of John Keble had been allowed briefly to survive her husband as a penance for keeping him from the Catholic Church.[5] Yet the conviction of Newman's sanctity is not confined to his co-religionists. Rendel Harris, the Quaker, said when he heard of his death, 'Now he belongs to the Church of all the saints.'

As a Roman Catholic, Newman was, as we all know, often disappointed and dispirited. There was much that repelled him, from Italianate piety to episcopal prevarications. He wished the Church of England might become more catholic and the Church of Rome more Christian. Yet he never repented of his 'second journey'. In the midst of a changing world and Victorian agnosticism, he felt that the only real choice was between the Catholic Church and atheism. Rome gave him the dogmatic security for which he craved and from which he could venture out to combat error and engage the more ardently in the quest for that truth which was once for all in Christ. Liberalism – the doctrine that one creed is as good as another – he still loathed, though there was, in Vidler's phrase, a greater 'liberality' than before. As an old man, he looked towards the time when 'the Latin race will not have a monopoly of the magisterium of Catholicism. We must be patient in our time; but God will take care of his Church – and when the hour strikes, the reform will begin.'[6]

Newman's vision was at least in part fulfilled by the Second Vatican Council. The coincidence between his teaching and that of the Council a century later suggests that we should recognize in him 'a sort of prophetic charisma'. And that prophetic charisma is seen in some of his final letters. In one he said that he felt, 'A silent and secret process is going on in the hearts of many . . . a definite work of Divine Providence . . . that would issue in a public opinion strong enough for the spread and exaltation of divine truth over all the world.'[7] It is a vision as yet unrealized. Indeed, it seems to recede as fundamentalism grows, reactionaries recover ground and Western Christendom succumbs to secularism. Yet the influence of religion does not diminish, as events in Eastern Europe and southern Africa illustrate. Newman's vision is one to keep before us. So too is his ecumenical generosity. He sees the divine hand laid upon 'the hearts and minds of many'. He stood for an ecumenism found in common aspirations rather than common documents.

He refused to become an assistant at the First Vatican Council and he would not have been at home in the creation of ecumenical instruments or the production of ecumenical reports, much as some of them could benefit from his style. In the end, his ecumenism lies in what Dean Church of St Paul's, whose Anglican friendship never failed him, described as 'bonds of affinity, subtler, more real and more prevailing than even the fatal legacies of the great schism'.[8] Newman was not surprised that Non-conformists bought the second edition of *Parochial and Plain Sermons*. He said that 'whatever tends to create a unity of heart between different communions lays the ground for advances towards a restoration of that visible unity, the absence of which amongst Christians is so great an advantage to the enemies of the cross'.[9]

In Newman there was always an underlying intuition which could hold together apparent contradictions. How can he help us to do the same?

1. He understood the value of *godly restraint*. He was a believer in *reserve*. He shrank from reducing faith to trivialized simplicities or from shouting sacred mysteries at street corners. He believed the

cross should be a constant image in our minds, and we should not talk of it easily to others, but rather be silent 'like the penitent woman, who showed her love in deep, subdued acts'.[10] Like Pascal, he knew that we live and die alone before God. And yet the royal banners go before us. We have saints, apostles, prophets, martyrs for company. This is what it means to believe in the Holy Catholic Church, the beloved community of those who lead each other to God in life and death and do so remembering Jesus.

2. *He took unbelief seriously*, both in himself and the world around him. F D Maurice said that Newman 'was governed by an infinite scepticism counteracted by an infinite devoutness'.[11] He reasoned his way to assent, finding passage to belief through the accumulation of probabilities, but in the end recognizing that a risk, indeed a leap of faith, has to be taken as the path to God. He is still a master in understanding the psychology of Christian conviction. Faith must be of the mind, for intellect is essential, but it must also be of the feelings. And there is also the moral sense. 'Revelation', he said in an Oxford sermon, 'was not given to satisfy our doubts, but to make us *better* men, and it is as we become better men that it becomes light and peace to our souls even though to the end of life we shall find difficulties in it and in the world around us.'[12]

3. Above all, Newman was an apostle of *holiness*. The young Richard Church was saved from rationalism in his Oxford days because he came into contact with Newman in whom 'the awfulness of things unseen was a present reality'.[13] The first of the published sermons was on the text, 'Holiness, without which no man shall see the Lord'. It is an austere sermon, yet insistent that 'inward sanctification is a condition different from our acceptance of the proffer of mercy and not negligently to be passed over in our thoughts as a necessary consequence of it'. He would not have made the mistake of thinking that holiness could be received in an instant. 'To obtain the gift of holiness is the work of a life.'[14]

4. Then, finally, there is a thread of *Providence* which leads us through the contradictions of his life. We see it the more clearly in retrospect. It is why, despite his changes of mind and allegiance, we can claim without strain that Newman belongs to us all, and somehow through him we belong to one another.

In a letter written to an Anglican priest towards the end of his life, Newman said,

> Those great burning truths, which I learned when a boy from evangelical teaching, I have found impressed upon my heart with fresh and ever-increasing force by the holy Roman Church. That Church has added to the simple evangelicalism of my first teachers, but it has obscured, diluted, enfeebled *nothing* of it . . .[15]

The basic affirmation of faith made by the schoolboy in 1816, that faith in the God revealed in Jesus Christ, was one with the affirmation of faith of the Cardinal in 1887. Newman's sense of the unity of his life and convictions has to be related to the importance he attached to memory in human life as a whole. He had himself a very vivid capacity for recalling his earlier years and he had an almost obsessive concern for the commemoration of personal and family anniversaries. In his room in the Oratory at Birmingham he kept a whole series of mementos to remind him of his years at Trinity, at Oriel and as vicar of this church. He lived his life under the sign of remembrance and thanksgiving, and just as in his Anglican days he had made use of the prayers of the Roman breviary, so at the end of his life as a cardinal the *Preces Privatae* of Launcelot Andrewes were still on his prayer desk.

This power of memory extended to the smallest details. Writing to Dean Church's daughter in 1876, thanking her for giving him a copy of *The Hunting of the Snark*, Newman recalls his 'thoughts and feelings . . . as I lay in my crib in the early spring, the cheerful song of the mower's scythe on the lawn . . . and how in coming downstairs slowly, for I brought down both feet on each step, I said to myself, "This is June!", though what my experience of June was, and how it was broad enough to be a matter of reflection, I really cannot tell'.[16]

Constantly Newman is fascinated by this feeling of the presence of the past. For him it is an essential element in the mystery of human personality, a kind of natural basis for his sense of God's constant, providential leading, which never left him. It was this which carried him through the experience of 1816, through his illness in Sicily in 1833, through the events which led up to 1845, and then on through the vicissitudes of his later life in Birmingham and Dublin, until the final vindication of the Cardinal's hat in 1879. And this personal pilgrimage through time was only part of the pilgrimage of the whole Church towards the Kingdom of God.

As the importance of John Henry Newman is more and more recognized in the Roman Catholic Church, this private and personal sense of continuity begins to assume a new and more public significance. Newman is seen increasingly as a representative figure in the nineteenth-century history of the Church. His journey of faith acquires a universal meaning. If for Anglicans the move he made in 1845 sets a question mark against the permanence of their position, perhaps for Roman Catholics his concern to maintain the unity between his earlier and later life demands a readiness to look more closely at where he came from.

The coming together of the Churches after centuries of separation is not something which can happen overnight. Ideas and convictions are things which, as Newman saw, take time to mature and to be realized. There is a need for 'chronic familiarity'. The arresting phrase is his. Pope John Paul spoke recently in our conversation in Rome of the need for an *affective* collegiality to grow into *effective* collegiality. At many different levels, and in a multitude of ways, the broken unity needs to be slowly restored, the underlying continuity recovered. In this process the person and teaching of Newman has a special place.

Pusey, writing in 1845 after Newman's conversion, refused to engage in old-fashioned anti-papalist invective, but instead saw the parting of friends as potent with new possibilities of unity: 'If anything could open their eyes to what is good in us, or soften in us any wrong prejudices against them, it would be the presence of such a one, nurtured to such rightness in our church, and now removed to theirs.'[17]

There is a unity in Newman's life. It is a sign of the unity of the human person, made in God's image and likeness. It is a unity restored in us as we respond to the revelation of the unity of God himself, revealed and declared in Jesus Christ. This same unity is God's gift and call to all his people, to his one holy, catholic and apostolic Church. It is as a witness to that unity in the cross and in the pilgrimage of the cross through history that Newman lived.

'For whoever would save his life will lose it and whoever loses his life for my sake and the gospel's will save it.'

NOTES

1. From J C Shairp, Professor of Humanity, St Andrews (1866), *John Keble*, pp. 12–17, quoted R W Church, *The Oxford Movement* (Macmillan 1892), pp. 141–3.
2. *Essay on the Development of Christian Doctrine* (Penguin 1974), p. 120.
3. ibid., p. 100.
4. *Apologia pro vita sua* (Sheed & Ward 1976), ch. 2, p. 33.
5. *Letters and Diaries of John Henry Newman*, ed. C S Dessain et al. (OUP 1973–7), XXII, p. 234.
6. LD XXV, pp. 326–7.
7. LD XXI, p. 181.
8. R W Church, *Occasional Paper II* (Macmillan 1897), p. 469.
9. LD XXIV, p. 22.
10. *Parochial and Plain Sermons* (Rivingtons 1882), V, p. 339.
11. Quoted by F J A Hort, in A F Hort, ed., *Life and Letters of Fenton J A Hort* (Macmillan 1896), p. 423.
12. *Parochial and Plain Sermons*, I, p. 229.
13. B A Smith, *Dean Church* (OUP 1958), pp. 235f.
14. *Parochial and Plain Sermons*, I, pp. 11, 12.
15. To George T Edwards, 24 February 1887; LD XXI, p. 189.
16. LD XXVIII, pp. 52–3.
17. Letter in *English Churchman* of 16 October 1845; quoted in *Life of Edward Bouverie Pusey*, ed. H P Liddon (Longman 1893), II, p. 461.

Index